Ingram
3/14/89
14.95

W9-BRF-662

Winnie Mandela

LIFE OF STRUGGLE

Winnie Mandela

LIFE OF STRUGGLE

Jim Haskins

G. P. PUTNAM'S SONS ▪ NEW YORK

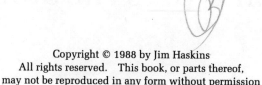

Book design by Gunta Alexander
Printed in the United States of America.
First impression

Library of Congress Cataloging-in-Publication Data

Haskins, 1941-   Winnie Mandela : life of struggle / Jim Haskins.   p.
cm. Bibliography: p.   Includes index.   Summary: Follows the life
of the woman who married a prominent leader for racial equality in
South Africa and then became an activist in that field herself.   1.
Mandela, Winnie—Juvenile literature. 2. Banned persons (South
Africa)—Biography—Juvenile literature. 3. Civil rights workers—South
Africa—Biography—Juvenile literature. 4. Anti-apartheid
movements—South Africa—Juvenile literature. 5. Mandela, Nelson,
1918-   —Juvenile literature.   [1. Mandela, Winnie. 2. Civil rights
workers. 3. Blacks—Biography. 4. South Africa—Race relations.] I.
Title.   DT779.955.M36H38 1988   968.06′092′4—dc19   [B[[92]
87-23725   CIP   AC
ISBN 0-399-21515-8

Photographs: between pages 74 and 75.

I am grateful to Ann Jefferies and Kathy Benson for their help in researching this project, and to Refna Wilkin, my editor, for her belief in it and her always superb suggestions.

To Annie

Winnie Mandela

LIFE OF STRUGGLE

Winnie
Mandela

LIFE OF STRUGGLE

Jim Haskins

G. P. PUTNAM'S SONS ▪ NEW YORK

Book design by Gunta Alexander
Printed in the United States of America.
First impression

Library of Congress Cataloging-in-Publication Data

Haskins, 1941-   Winnie Mandela : life of struggle / Jim Haskins.   p.
cm. Bibliography: p.   Includes index.   Summary: Follows the life
of the woman who married a prominent leader for racial equality in
South Africa and then became an activist in that field herself.   1.
Mandela, Winnie—Juvenile literature. 2. Banned persons (South
Africa)—Biography—Juvenile literature. 3. Civil rights workers—South
Africa—Biography—Juvenile literature. 4. Anti-apartheid
movements—South Africa—Juvenile literature. 5. Mandela, Nelson,
1918-   —Juvenile literature.   [1. Mandela, Winnie. 2. Civil rights
workers. 3. Blacks—Biography. 4. South Africa—Race relations.] I.
Title.   DT779.955.M36H38 1988   968.06'092'4—dc19   [B[[92]
87-23725   CIP   AC
ISBN 0-399-21515-8

Photographs: between pages 74 and 75.

I am grateful to Ann Jefferies and Kathy Benson for their help in researching this project, and to Refna Wilkin, my editor, for her belief in it and her always superb suggestions.

To Annie

Contents

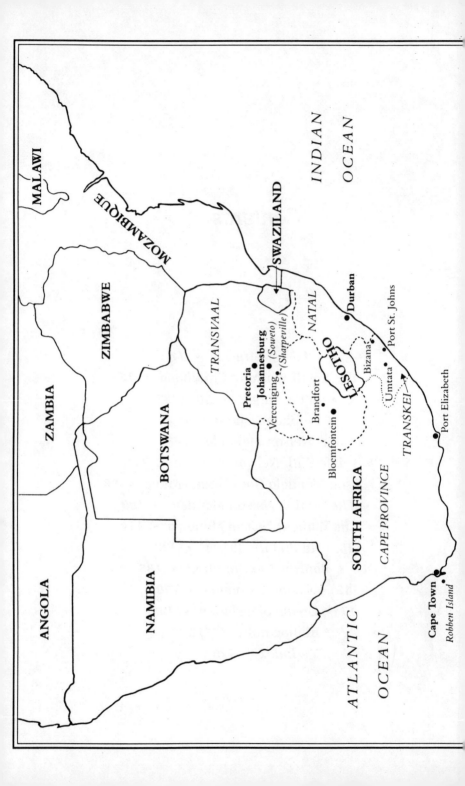

Winnie Mandela

LIFE OF STRUGGLE

·1·

Life of Struggle

On December 3, 1985, a huge rally was held in Mamelodi, a black township outside Pretoria in South Africa. The occasion was the funeral of twelve blacks who had been killed during a clash with police three weeks earlier; one of the twelve was a two-month-old baby who had suffocated to death from tear-gas fumes. More than 40,000 people packed the Mamelodi soccer stadium, including diplomats from the United States and ten other Western countries. The mostly black crowd cheered the speeches by both black and white speakers against apartheid, the system of complete racial segregation in South Africa. They sang freedom songs and waved the black, green, and gold flag of the outlawed African National Congress. Then they started leaving to go home.

Fewer than 10,000 were still in the stadium when Winnie Mandela arrived. They were astonished to see the wife of Nelson Mandela, the leader of the African National Congress, who has been imprisoned for more than twenty years. Winnie Mandela was a banned person.

The system of banning in South Africa is a unique one, under which the government can severely restrict a person's activities. Without bringing any charges or offering any proof, the government can deny someone the right to meet with more than two other people even at home, to attend public gatherings, speak in public, write any book or article or pamphlet. The government can deny a person the right to live in his or her own home, to travel freely, to visit friends or relatives. A banned person has no right to appeal such banning orders.

As a banned person, Winnie Mandela was not supposed to attend large gatherings. She was certainly not supposed to address them. But Winnie did. Wearing on her head a scarf in the black, green, and gold colors of the African National Congress, she stepped to the speakers' platform and told the crowd, "This is our country. As you have had to bury your children today, so shall the blood of these heroes be avenged."

The crowd went wild and began to chant her name, and Winnie smiled and waved. Then she left. The security police, who were everywhere, could have arrested her for defying her banning orders, but they did not. Winnie was not surprised. At the age of forty-nine, and having spent decades enduring police harassment, she had developed a very finely tuned sense of what she could and could not do in South Africa. She chose very carefully the public appearances she made and the public actions she took, for each one had to count. With her husband in prison and unable to speak to his people, she had to carry the banner of the dream of nationhood for black South Africans, inspiring her people and yet not challenging the white authorities so grievously that she, too, would end up in prison.

The most she could do was make a few, carefully selected public appearances. The government would not allow her to be quoted in South African newspapers. On Friday, December 13, ten days after the Mamelodi funeral, the government prohibited the sale or even the possession of her autobiography, *Part of My Soul Went With Him*, which had been published in West Germany and Canada the previous year, and in the United States in 1985. The South African censorship board found the book to be "undesirable."

Three days after that, the ruling white Afrikaners, descendants of the Dutch, German, and French Huguenot farmers who first arrived in South Africa in the 1650s, celebrated the Day of the Covenant. On that day 147 years before, a small group of whites had beaten 10,000 Zulu warriors after making a covenant with God, and they regarded their victory as proof that God meant them to rule the country. In South Africa, the Day of the Covenant is a national holiday, but the blacks who make up 85 percent of the population do not celebrate. For them, it is a day of sadness, a powerful ritual reminder of their oppression.

Black South Africans are among the most oppressed people in the world. They are forced to live under apartheid, a rigid system of separation of the races that segregates and discriminates against all nonwhite South Africans but which is especially harsh on blacks. They cannot choose where they want to live or work or how their children will be educated. In spite of the fact that they are in the vast majority in South Africa, they are powerless to directly change the attitude of the government. For a black in South Africa, even basic human dignity is something that must be fought for, and those who have had the courage to undertake this fight have invited the full fury of a brutal and repressive government. Winnie Mandela is one of these South African blacks.

She has refused to be bowed and has won worldwide respect and admiration. But she has paid a heavy price. In one way or another, her entire life has been a struggle against the apartheid system, first for herself and her family, and later for her people. For a black in South Africa, especially a black woman, this struggle and the courage to keep at it are remarkable. But Winnie Mandela is a remarkable woman.

· 2 ·

The Small World of Childhood

*W*innie Mandela was twelve years old before she realized that there were people with a different last name than hers. Until that time she had never been introduced to anyone who was not a Madikizela, and so naturally she thought that everyone had the same last name as she did.

It isn't hard to understand how this happened. It had been the tradition of her people, the Xhosa-speaking Nguni, for a man to have as many wives as he could afford. Her grandfather had had twenty-nine wives, and children with them all, and the sons had brought their wives back to the family home. When a kraal, or family compound, became too large, a group would travel a few miles away to form a new settlement of Madikizelas. By the time Winnie was born, there were six such Madikizela settlements in Eastern Pondoland, which took its name from the Pondo, to which Winnie's family belonged.

Winnie's village was called eMbongweni. Everyone in it was a Madikizela or related by marriage. In her own household there were between twenty and thirty children and three generations. Her family compound was like a miniature village itself, with a group of eight grass-roofed huts clustered around a T-shaped brick building where her father slept.

Winnie's father, Columbus Madikizela, was a member of the Methodist church, which did not believe in having more than one wife at a time. So Columbus had a much smaller family than his own father had had. He and his wife, Gertrude, had nine children. Winnie was the fifth.

She was born on September 26, 1936, and named Nomzamo, which means "trial" (not in the sense of a courtroom but in the sense of having a hard time in life) in Xhosa. Her birth was not officially recorded, for the South African State had no interest in the births of black babies in what it considered to be one of the most undeveloped areas of South Africa. She was given the name Winifred when she was christened in the Methodist church because her parents, as Christians, believed in Christian names. Winifred is a German name, for her father believed the German people were hardworking and admired them for that. Winnie is the name by which she is known to the outside world.

Her parents were very strict with their children. Her mother, Gertrude, was deeply religious and had very strong ideas about how children should behave. Winnie and her brothers and sisters were expected to pray three times a day. Sometimes they did so locked in a room with their mother. At other times they went to a corner of the garden where the high grass formed a protective shelter. Naturally, they went to church every Sunday. Their mother, who had perhaps heard the maxim that cleanliness is next to godliness, also insisted that her children keep themselves immaculately clean. Each evening they lined up for inspection to make sure they had bathed and cleaned their teeth thoroughly. Every child who could walk had small chores to do.

Winnie's father had less contact with the children than her mother did, which was part of their culture. He slept apart from the rest of the family in the separate brick building. He did not often speak to them, and the children did not usually speak to him unless their mother was present. But there was no question that he, too, expected much from them, particularly as regarded their behavior and their education.

Columbus Madikizela was a teacher, the only teacher at the eMbongweni Primary School. Gertrude Madikizela had also trained to be a teacher and was the first domestic science teacher in the Bizana district when she and Columbus met. After their marriage, she had stopped working in order to have a family. Among Columbus' most prized possessions were hundreds of books, which he kept in the one-room stone house that served as his school office and in his brick house. He used them to teach his students history and math, natural science and English.

Columbus Madikizela was also an important man outside the village of eMbongweni. In fact, he could have been a chief if he had wanted. He was descended from a long line of chiefs and could have claimed that hereditary position. But in 20th century South Africa, chiefs had little power, being subservient to white administrators, even junior clerks. Columbus Madikizela had declined that hereditary position and had chosen instead to teach, but he was still active in regional affairs. He represented his region, Eastern Pondoland, in the territorial council that met in the town of Umtata to pass laws for all the blacks of the Transkei. He also acted as interpreter when the local courts met, for the white rulers of South Africa insisted on white magistrates presiding at these courts, and they needed someone who was fluent in both English and Xhosa to interpret for them.

When Winnie was born, South Africa was part of the British Empire, although from the late 1920s to the early 1930s, it had, basically, functioned as an independent nation. For many years before that, South Africa had been under the control of Great Britain, but the British had been only the latest in a series of white European groups to arrive and to dominate Southern Africa.

First there were the Portuguese, who rounded the tip of the continent as they searched for a sea route to India in the late 1400s. They were interested in the ivory and the gold and other minerals they found, and they built trading posts, which eventually became settlements, in the areas of present-day Angola, Mozambique, and elsewhere. They sought to bring Christianity and Western education to the native Africans, but at the same time Portuguese slave traders were engaging in a brisk business in human beings. Concentrated primarily on the West Coast of Africa, the slave trade grew quickly, as the need increased for laborers in the Portuguese colonies in the far-off West Indies and Brazil. Slavery was practiced by the native Africans in West Africa and West Central Africa, and the local chiefs traded slaves to the Portuguese in return for European goods.

The area of present-day South Africa was first colonized by the Dutch, who arrived in 1652. They too were mainly interested in the spices and other riches of India; the out-post the Dutch East India Company established at the Cape of Good Hope was at first only a stopping point, a place to take on fresh water and supplies, during the long sea voyage from Holland to India.

Most Dutch people were perfectly happy in their own country and did not care to be pioneers in a strange land, so the Dutch East India Company brought in French Huguenots, who had been forced to leave France because of their religious beliefs. They, and a few Germans and Dutch, were the majority of white settlers in the Cape area. Many of them were indentured servants who had agreed to work a certain number of years for the company in return for their eventual freedom.

After a time, the indentured servants hired by the company to work at the outpost asked for and received their freedom to become farmers and cattle raisers. When their farms and herds became too large for them to handle alone, and the native Khoi and San peoples (sometimes referred to together as the Khoisan), who lived in the Cape area, were reluctant to work for them, they imported slaves from East Africa, Madagascar, Ceylon, India, and Malaya. By the turn of the century, these slaves made up over half the population of the Cape Province, which was estimated at 33,000. The local Khoi, whom the European settlers called Hottentots, and the San, called Bushmen, were not among these slaves. They did not practice slavery and did not engage in the trading of slaves. And since the Dutch depended on the Khoisan for the cattle trade, they had banned the enslavement of these people from the first.

The intermingling of both the early white settlers and

the native blacks with the slaves created the first Coloureds, or mixed-race peoples.

The British were the next group to arrive from Europe. They were invited by the Dutch prince of Orange, who fled his own country when the Dutch replaced their monarchy with a republic in 1795. He asked the British to take over his colonies and look after them until he could regain his throne, and that same year the British sent troops to occupy the Cape Colony. In 1814 the former Dutch colonies in Africa came officially under British control. Over the next twenty years, thousands of British settlers arrived in Southern Africa—5,000 in 1820 alone. The Afrikaners—the descendants of the early Dutch, German, and French Huguenot settlers—resented the English. They later called the 19th century the Century of Wrong. They resisted the imposition of English as the official language. But they resented most of all the fact that the British had abolished the slave trade and in 1833 freed all who were slaves. But both the British and the Afrikaners regarded nonwhites as inferior, and the 19th century was just another century of wrong for black Africans.

At her father's school, Winnie learned to read and speak English fluently. She also learned far more history than most black African children, for it was her father's favorite subject and he spent a great deal of time teaching it to his students at the eMbongweni Primary School. Many of his personal books were about history, and he used them in his teachings more often than he used the books that were part of the official curriculum drawn up by the white Cape Education Department. He felt that the official texts were woefully lacking, especially in history. They told history from the white point of view and barely mentioned the history of black South Africans. Winnie said years later, "I remember distinctly . . . how he taught us about the nine Xhosa wars. Of course we had textbooks, naturally written by white men, and they had their interpretation, why there were nine 'Kaffir' wars [Kaffir is used disparagingly, like Nigger]. Then he would put the textbook aside and say: 'Now this is what the book says, but the truth is: these white people invaded our country and stole the land from our grandfathers. The clashes between white and black were originally the result of cattle thefts. The whites took the cattle and the blacks would go and fetch them back.'"

Columbus Madikizela also preferred to teach his pupils a kind of history that would make them proud of their own heritage, and there was much to be proud of. Long before the arrival of white settlers from Europe there were advanced civilizations in Africa, with organized governments, standing armies, and complicated trade arrangements. Archeologists have found prehistoric gold and copper mines as well as the remains of huge stone castles and entire walled cities. There is evidence, too, although it is somewhat controversial, that Africans traveled across the Atlantic to carry on trade with the Western Hemisphere Indians before Columbus, for the first Spanish and Portuguese explorers found colonies of black men on the eastern coasts of Central and South America. Africa is the cradle of humanity. Indeed, the oldest dated rock art (20,000 B.C.) has been found in Southern Africa.

While she learned history in one way from her father at school, Winnie learned history in yet another way at home, from her grandmother. In the strong oral tradition in African culture, older people considered it their duty to pass on the history of their tribe and their family to younger people, and Winnie's grandmother took her responsibility seriously. At night, the entire household gathered around blazing log fires, and while the children ate sour milk and mealie-meal, the old men and women told them stories.

Many of the stories were myths and legends about spirits and demons that inhabited the woods and the trees, the rocks, and the rivers. Such beliefs were frowned upon by the Christian faith, and practicing Christians like Columbus and Gertrude Madikizela had mixed feelings about letting their children listen to them. But these myths and legends were part of the history of their people, and they wanted their children to grow up knowing about their heritage.

Other stories were not myths at all, but reports, handed down from generation to generation, about how the white settlers had come and disrupted the lives of the Xhosa-speaking peoples, including the Pondo. The Xhosa, Tembu, Pondo, and other closely related groups had been living in southeast Africa since at least the 1200s and possibly even earlier, long before the Portuguese or Dutch or British came to Southern Africa. For many years after the arrival of these settlers, the Xhosa had been left in peace, for they were far enough away from the Cape and the other early settlements to be left undisturbed.

But beginning in the early 1800s European settlers had started a great expansion, pushing the frontier closer and closer to the Xhosa settlements in the area now called the Transkei, taking their land and their cattle. The Xhosa fought back and there were nine major "Xhosa wars," in 1811, 1819, 1834, and 1846, in addition to a few minor skirmishes, all of which saw the Xhosa defeated by the European guns and horses. By 1850 the Xhosa had acquired and learned how to use guns themselves, and managed to hold back the invaders for a time. But once again they lost.

Some Xhosa who claimed to be able to forecast the future had long suggested that if the people destroyed their own crops and cattle, their ancestors would rise up from their graves and drive the white man to the sea. By 1857, the Xhosa were exhausted from fighting wars, and the ranks of their warriors were thin. They decided to believe the prophecies and slaughtered their cattle and destroyed their crops. But no ancestors arose to save them. Tens of thousands died of starvation in the Transkei. Tens of thousands more left the Transkei in search of food and work. About twenty years later, in 1878–1879, the Xhosa tried one last major war of resistance, but after being defeated in that series of battles they gave up. Gradually the British took over the territories; Pondoland was the last to be incorporated into the Cape Colony in 1894.

Around the same time, an increasing number of people in the Transkeian Territories began to turn to Christianity, perhaps because they felt their own beliefs had failed them.

When Winnie's grandmother spoke of the arrival of the white man, she described him as carrying two things: a Bible and a "button" (her word for money). Both, she understood, were powerful weapons against the Xhosa culture. The Bible contained beliefs that were different from those held by the Xhosa, and if they were to believe in what was written in the Bible, then they had to give up their old beliefs.

Money was equally powerful. The Xhosa had not needed it before the white men came. They had objects of value, but their custom was to trade one object of value for another. Under the British, they suddenly found that they needed money. That was the only thing the British would accept as payment for the taxes they imposed. And they imposed those taxes to be paid in the form of money to force the native Africans to work for them in order to earn money. That was a very clever way to persuade the Africans to go to the British towns to work. It was also a very clever way to get the Xhosa away from their farms and their cattle herds.

Winnie's grandmother had never seen a white person, but she had heard descriptions, and she described their pale skins and light-colored eyes and long, straight hair as if she knew them well. She knew them, and she hated them for destroying her people's culture and stealing their lands and their cattle. Even now, they were threatening the greatest source of wealth of the Pondo with new destocking laws that the government said would reduce a serious problem of overstocking on the velds (open fields) of the Transkei. The Pondo believed the laws were really aimed at opening up more of the lands to white farmers and at reducing the wealth of the Pondo so they would be forced to go to work for the farmers. Her grandmother's attitude toward whites was Winnie's first experience of racial hatred, and it made a deep impression on her. "There is an anger that wakes up in you as a child," she has said. "You tell yourself: 'If they failed in those nine Xhosa wars, I am one of them and I will start from where those Xhosa left off and get my land back.'" But she was far too young to understand racism, and even the history that her grandmother told was no different in her young mind from the myths of spirits and demons. She was a child, and since she had enough to eat and a strong and protective family, she really had no idea what it meant to be deprived of land or cattle or culture.

Compared with other Pondo children growing up in the Transkei, indeed, compared with the vast majority of black South Africans, Winnie had a comfortable childhood. In addition to drawing a salary for his job teaching, her father grew vegetables and kept cattle, and there was always enough to eat. At the main midday meal and again at the lighter evening meal, Winnie and the other children gathered around large enamel dishes, several to each dish, and ate together from them. Only when they were older did each child get a plate.

There was also money for the compulsory school fees that all black children had to pay (in South Africa, education was free only for white children), and for uniforms. That those uniforms did not include shoes did not bother Winnie. None of the children wore shoes; they ran around barefoot summer and winter, and this made sense given that the floors of their sleeping huts as well as of the huts which served as their classrooms were of dirt smeared with cow dung. Even the meticulous Gertrude Madikizela would have been hard-pressed to keep her children's shoes clean and polished under such circumstances.

Winnie was something of a tomboy who loved to run fast as the wind and to climb trees and who was more interested in what her brothers, Christopher and Lungile, were doing, than in girls' activities. She even preferred wearing Christopher and Lungile's hand-me-down shirts and pants to her older sister's clothes. At an early age she was assertive and always chose the activities for herself and her older sister, Nancy, with whom she was very close. She even had the courage to speak up to her father on occasion, but because it was in compassion he did not disapprove. She realized that some of her schoolmates had not returned to school, and when she learned that it was because their parents could not afford the compulsory fees, she pleaded with her father to pay the fees out of his own pocket. He finally agreed to do so.

She excelled at school. When inspectors from the Cape Education Department visited, she was chosen to recite the English and arithmetic oral examinations for them. All the children of Columbus and Gertrude Madikizela were expected to do well in their studies, and the plan was for all of them to continue at boarding school once they had completed their years at eMbongweni Primary School. But of the girls, Winnie showed the greatest promise. She has explained that this was partly due to her need to show her mother, who had a marked preference for sons, that girls were as good as boys. "I remember her asking God every day for a son," Winnie has recalled. "This . . . developed in me the feeling, I will prove to her that a girl is as much of value to a parent as a son." This may also have been one reason why Winnie was a tomboy and preferred boys' clothes and boys' activities.

Even though Gertrude Madikizela favored boys, she loved all her children dearly. Winnie came to understand this during the first family tragedy that she can remember. Winnie's older sister, Vuyelwa, who was away at boarding school in nearby Bizana, returned home ill with tuberculosis. Winnie's mother did all she could to nurse her daughter back to health, but there was no hospital and no professional doctor in the district. Gertrude Madikizela prayed for her sick child as she had never prayed before, but Vuyelwa died anyway. Winnie was only seven years old when she stood beside her sister's bed and watched her father pull a white sheet over the small body. She wondered why her sister had died after all her mother's praying.

Winnie's mother was never quite the same after that. Winnie remembered that she seemed to grow smaller as the days went by, wasting away either from the same disease that had taken Vuyelwa or from cancer (Winnie is not sure which). She sat in the dark corners of the house praying, but once again the prayers did no good. Winnie had not yet reached her ninth birthday when her mother died as well.

Gertrude Madikizela had been the family's center, and the household was in turmoil after her death. Aunts came to help, but they were poor stand-ins. Winnie, who had been a fearless child, was suddenly overtaken by panic. At night she would lie awake shivering in fright, and when she finally slept she had terrible nightmares. Her safe little world was shattered, the orderly rhythms of life as she had known it were gone.

Life for the family would never be quite the same after that, but after a time its members settled into a new routine. Columbus Madikizela put aside his own grief when he realized that the children needed some sort of anchor. Usually when a mother died, the children were sent to live with aunts, but Columbus decided instead to keep his children with him and to raise them himself. There were four boys—Christopher, Lungile, Thanduxolo, and Msuthu—and four girls—Nancy, Winnie, Nikiwe Xaba, and Nonyaniso. Those who were able (the youngest child was still a baby) took on various household duties, and as time went on the family reassembled itself.

Those were hard years, though, and not just because of the loss of Gertrude. World War II was raging, and many young men in the district had volunteered to fight in the South African army. The Afrikaners in power rather reluctantly decided to aid the British against the Germans, and both black and white South Africans fought the German General Erwin Rommel in Egypt in North Africa. The black soldiers, however, were not allowed to carry guns and had to fight against Rommel's tanks and artillery with spears. Many were killed. As the war went on, especially in remote places like the Transkei, there were shortages of things like sugar and soap, and even in remote Transkei the war was ever present in the reports about local men who had died in battle.

When the war finally ended in 1945, there was great rejoicing and a big celebration at Town Hall in nearby Bizana. Winnie and the other children of eMbongweni begged to be allowed to attend the celebration, and their parents gave permission. But when they arrived at the Town Hall, they were barred from entering: the festivities were only for whites. As Winnie pressed her nose against a window and watched the white children and their parents eating and celebrating, she began to understand her grandmother's hatred of the whites.

Three years later she received her second lesson in white power and black powerlessness. She was two months into Standard Six, the highest grade in eMbongweni Primary School, when her father sadly informed her that he'd been ordered to close down Standard Six altogether. The Cape Department of Education said his school was overcrowded and that from then on the school would go only through Standard Five. Those students in Standard Six were to be transferred to school elsewhere. The trouble was that the closest schools, those in Bizana and the nearby village of Ndunge, were overcrowded, too, and had no more room. Two months into Standard Six, Winnie had no place to go.

Her father did not take her back into Standard Five at eMbongweni Primary School. Instead, he asked her to go to work on his lands, milking cows, picking crops, and even plowing fields. Winnie did not feel it was right to question him about his decision and so did not know if he might have behaved differently if she had been a son rather than a daughter. It occurred to her that he might be testing her obedience, and she proved equal to the test. She did her farm work as she had been asked, and at night read the lessons she would have been receiving at school.

Fall turned into winter on the Transkei velds (the seasons in South Africa are the opposite of those in North America), and Winnie tried not to think about how much school she was missing as her brothers and sisters returned home from Bizana and Ndunge on the holidays that separated the four parts of the South African school year. Then, in August, as winter drew to a close, one of her sisters came home ill (thankfully, her illness was not fatal) and Winnie's father told Winnie that she would go to school in her sister's place. In September she traveled to the village of Ndunge to resume her schooling.

Since Ndunge was too far away from eMbongweni to travel to every day, for the first time in her life Winnie was away from home. But she stayed with her grandparents on her mother's side, so it was not as if she had to live with strangers. Actually, she liked the idea of being away from home and regarded it as a sign of growing up. It was not being away from home that worried her, but having been away from school for five months. At first she was afraid that she would be unable to catch up with the rest of the class. But she soon realized that she was ahead of most of the other Standard Six pupils. Apparently, the Cape Education Department was not too concerned about overcrowding in Ndunge, for there were 200 students in her class alone, divided into three groups of about seventy each. When she arrived, they were just about to take their last major tests preceding the end-of-the-year examinations, and Winnie, who had not taken a test in several months, was relieved when she learned that she had passed. At the end of the year, she was one of only twenty-two who passed her external Standard Six examinations.

She was now eligible to enter secondary school, and there was no question that she would go. The majority of black children in South Africa never went past Standard Six, even if their parents had the money for secondary-school fees and uniforms. Schooling for them was inadequate, teachers were less well-trained, most of their classrooms did not even have desks and chairs, and yet they were expected to pass the same examinations as the white children, who paid no fees and had all the books and furniture and well-trained teachers they needed. Not only had Winnie overcome the usual obstacles to a black child's getting an education, she had also overcome a five-month forced "holiday" from school. She deserved to go on to secondary school, and her father was delighted to pay the fees.

She would attend Bizana Secondary School and for the first time in her life she would not be living with relatives. Also, for the first time in her life she would wear shoes.

And so, the small childhood world of Nomzamo Winnie Madikizela was expanding. From the safe and protected family in a village where everyone was a Madikizela she had moved to another village where there were actually people with different last names. Now she was going to a real town where there were people from other places, and where there were whites as well as blacks. She had no way of knowing, then, how large and hostile was the world that lay beyond.

▪3▪

In the
Larger World

Before Winnie even set foot in Bizana Secondary School she experienced the brutal side of the larger world she was entering. The stores, like the other businesses in Bizana, were owned and operated by whites, although most of their customers were blacks. They catered especially to the people who lived in the rural areas, where there were no stores, and who often journeyed long distances to Bizana for things like sugar and other items that they could not grow in their gardens. In one such store where Winnie and her father stopped to buy food, Winnie saw the young white clerk kick and scream at a family of three when the father knelt down and broke a loaf of bread open to feed his wife and infant. The clerk called them Kaffirs and screamed that he would not have them soiling his store. Winnie was shocked at this brutality and looked up at her father, expecting him to intervene. But her father did nothing, and she was surprised and ashamed. He had always stood against violence and had never once raised a hand against any of his children. How could he let such an unfair thing happen and do nothing about it? But neither he nor any of the other blacks in the store did or said a thing.

Winnie knew it was not her place to ask her father why, but she wondered for a long time afterward about the incident. Much later she would understand that he was powerless to do anything, but she never forgot the incident, nor her shame that her father had done nothing. She remembered the times back at eMbongweni Primary School when the white education officials had visited, and how shabby her father looked in comparison to them. She had felt a sense of shame then as well, and resentment against the whites.

The rest of their shopping trip was more pleasant. Winnie's father bought her shoes, which felt strange on her callused feet, a black and white uniform, and a coat. Still a tomboy who was accustomed to wearing boy's clothes, she chose a man's overcoat several sizes too large, and her father bought it for her, feeling that she deserved to have what she wanted. Her classmates at Bizana Secondary School laughed at her in that coat, but she did not care; she felt safe in its large folds and sometimes wore it even when the weather was too warm for a coat.

At school, Winnie once again found that she could easily master the material she was taught, and proudly reported to her father after passing each set of examinations. While he was pleased with her progress, Columbus Madikizela was also becoming worried about just what she would do with her schooling. There were very few career choices for an educated black girl. She could become a teacher of black children, of course, but her father wanted her to strive to reach an even higher goal. When he learned that a college in Johannesburg had introduced a new course for blacks in medical social work, he knew he had the answer to his and Winnie's problem—she would become one of the first black medical social workers in South Africa.

Of course he realized that there was still competition for entrance into that course of study—black students from all over the country would be applying to the school. Winnie would have to pass the university entrance exams with very high marks in order to have a chance. He did not feel that Bizana Secondary School was tough enough to prepare her. A church-run school would be better for her. When Winnie returned home to tell her father that she had passed her Junior Certificate examinations, he told her that she would not be going back to Bizana. Instead, she would attend Shawbury High School in Qumbu. It was operated by the Methodist Mission, and most of its teachers, who were black, were college graduates, something which could not be said of the majority of black secondary school teachers in South Africa. Winnie's father believed that the courses at Shawbury would be more rigorous than at Bizana and prepare her better for the university entrance examinations.

It would be a financial struggle for Columbus to pay Winnie's tuition and living expenses at Shawbury, and Winnie wished that there was a way to help. But there was little help she could give. There were no scholarships available for black students at secondary schools in South Africa, and she was too young to get a job. Even if she had been old enough to work, her father would have refused to let her do so, for the whole purpose in sending her to Shawbury was for her to study. Realizing this, Winnie's older sister, Nancy, offered to leave boarding school herself in order to help the financial situation at home. Her father consented and Winnie was touched by the generosity of her sister. She promised to repay Nancy for her sacrifice as soon as she was able. This gesture was by no means unique. Cases like this are common among blacks in South Africa.

Winnie thrived at Shawbury, enjoying the challenge of the more demanding curriculum. She made friends easily and was popular with her schoolmates. She was shy but friendly and always willing to help others. What little pocket money she had, she would share. She helped younger girls with their lessons. She exchanged uniforms with girls of her size so it would not seem that she, and they, only had one school uniform. She was fifteen years old when she enrolled at the school and feeling very grown up and independent as each time she changed schools she moved a little farther away from her home village of eMbongweni. While she had yet to leave the Transkei, at Shawbury her awareness of the larger world increased greatly, and not just because of the courses in geography.

Most of the teachers at Shawbury were graduates of Fort Hare African University College in Alice, a town in the Eastern Cape, now located in the "homeland" of Ciskei, which grew up around a mission station established in 1824. Founded in 1916 and the only university college especially for blacks, it had attracted some of the brightest students from across the country and served as a caldron for their ideas about South Africa and black South African nationalism. Many future black leaders attended Fort Hare, including Robert Mugabe, now president of Zimbabwe, Robert Sobukwe, who would become a leader of the Pan African Congress, and Nelson Mandela and Oliver Tambo, leaders of the African National Congress. From the late 1930s on, it had been a place of great student political activism, and the graduates who went to Shawbury to teach took that activism with them. Many of them belonged to an organization called the Society of Young Africa, which was actually more scholarly than activist and quite distant from the masses of uneducated black people. But it was the first political organization of any kind that Winnie and her classmates had come into contact with, and the students were very impressed.

Winnie now learned more about the politics of South Africa, especially about the differences between the two groups of whites who held power, the English and the Afrikaners, and about the great changes that were taking place now that Afrikaner Nationalists were gaining power.

Back at eMbongweni Primary School, Winnie had learned the basic outlines of Afrikaner history in South Africa. She had learned that after the English took over the Dutch colony in the early 1800s, the descendants of the first Dutch, German, and French settlers, who called themselves Boers (farmers) or Afrikaners (after Afrikaans, the Dutch-derived language they spoke), had resented the English attempt to change their laws and customs and to make English the official language. In fact, by 1834 about 10 percent of the Afrikaners had decided they'd had enough and that the only thing to do was to put as much distance as they could between themselves and the British.

In that year, four to six thousand men and women left

their homes, loaded their prized possessions onto ox-drawn wagons, and began a slow and difficult journey northward. They had no clear destination, they only knew they wanted to leave the English as far behind as possible and to find a land where they could live in peace. Over the next four years they encountered many hostile groups of Africans, and countless times had to draw their wagons into a circle to defend themselves. Each time, they survived and pressed onward. After a while, disputes broke out among them over which way to go, and groups splintered off in several directions.

One group managed to get across the Drakensberg Mountains to the area of Natal, which was ruled by the Zulu. They asked to be allowed to settle there, and at first the Zulu chief, Dingane, agreed to let them settle in the area, but then he changed his mind. When seventy Voortrekkers (journeyers) arrived at his compound to sign the treaty they had negotiated, he ordered his men to slaughter them all.

The survivors of this massacre got word to another group of Voortrekkers, and several months later a small but determined force of Boers, led by a man named Andries Pretorius, arrived to do battle against Dingane and his 10,000 warriors. On December 16, 1838, before they went into battle, Pretorius and his men knelt down and made a covenant, or pact, with God: if He would help them win the coming battle, they would forever after keep that day as a Day of Thanksgiving in His honor. In the battle that followed, called the Battle of Blood River, the Voortrekkers were astonishingly victorious, losing only a handful of men compared to the 3,000 Zulus they killed. They took over Natal and established the first Boer republic, firm in the belief that they were a people chosen by God to live and prosper there. Every year afterward, they celebrated the Day of the Covenant.

Four years later, Britain took control of Natal, but the Boers proved to be so resistant that eventually the British let them have two republics: the Transvaal and the Orange Free State. The British held on to Natal and the two groups coexisted.

Then, in 1868, diamonds were discovered in the Orange Free State, and the British decided they would like that area after all. By 1877 they had also decided to take over the Transvaal, and in that year the first Boer War broke out. The Boers won, and retook control of the Transvaal. Then gold was discovered in the Transvaal, once again the British tried to take control, and there was a second Boer War. This one lasted nearly three years, but the British eventually won in 1902, after inventing some gruesome techniques like barbed wire and concentration camps. Eight years later, the British agreed to form the Union of South Africa, a self-governing dominion within the British Empire made up of the Transvaal, the Orange Free State, Natal, and the Cape Province.

Now that they had secured self-government, the white South Africans wasted no time establishing laws to ensure that they would control the fertile and mineral-rich lands and have an unlimited supply of black labor on the farms and in the mines.

One of the worst and most far-reaching of these laws was the 1913 Natives' Land Act. This, combined with the Natives' Trust and Lands Act of 1936, the year Winnie was born, set aside about 12 or 13 percent of South Africa's lands for more than 4,000,000 blacks and about 87 percent for the 1,250,000 whites. These acts also put African tenant farmers and sharecroppers on white farms on a wage-earning basis, meaning that they worked directly for the whites instead of partly for themselves. With the mass dislocations called for in order to move the Africans off the lands reserved for whites, the authorities also ensured an even greater labor supply, for where were the blacks to go if not to work for whites?

Then there were the master-and-servant laws and the pass laws, which required all nonwhites to carry identification books. If Africans were caught without them, or if the books were not in order, they could be arrested and jailed.

Also in the early 1900s, laws were passed against other nonwhite groups in South Africa, including the sizeable Indian population which had arisen from the Indian laborers that the British had brought into Natal to work on the sugar plantations in 1860. Led by Mohandas K. Gandhi, who later became famous for his nonviolent campaign against the British in India, the Indians mounted large-scale passive resistance campaigns against anti-Indian legislation in 1907 and again in 1913–1914.

Coloureds, too, resisted these laws. Coloureds were the products of marital and nonmarital relationships between whites and blacks that had gone on since the first whites had arrived. By the early 1900s they were a large group, especially in the Cape area. In 1902 they formed the African Political (later People's) Organization, the first nonwhite large political organization, but achieved only limited success.

The strongest political organization to be formed around that time was the South African Native National

Congress, which was founded by four young lawyers led by Pixley ka Izaka Seme. He had just returned from studying at Columbia University in the United States and at Oxford University in England, and in its formative years the organization was influenced by the ideas of W.E.B. DuBois, a black American, and of Marcus Garvey, a black British West Indian. DuBois and Garvey believed in and worked for the idea of Pan-Africanism, the unity of black cultures across geographical boundaries. By 1917 the leaders of the South African Native National Congress had adopted this larger view of their struggle and changed the name of the organization to the African National Congress (ANC). Its purpose was to overcome tribal divisions and to present unified demands for industrial education, the right to own land, and some form of representation in Parliament. Its anthem, written by a Xhosa composer, was titled "Nkosi Sikelel' . . . iAfrica" ("Lord Bless Africa"). Its flag, adopted in 1925, consisted of three horizontal stripes: black for the people, green for the land, and gold for the country's resources. But they were not antiwhite, and from the beginning they made it clear that they would not be racists. For more than twenty years the ANC tried to bring about peaceful change through petitions and nonviolent demonstrations. But even these mild forms of protest were met with politicial repression and police violence. By the 1930s the ANC had temporarily lost its momentum.

In 1938, one hundred years after the Boer Great Trek, there was a surge in Afrikaner pride. In August, nine ox-drawn wagons retraced the route from Cape Town to Pretoria. They arrived on schedule on December 16, the one hundredth anniversary of the Day of the Covenant, and laid a stone monument at the spot where Pretorius had made the covenant with God. Afrikaners across the country were reminded that they were supposed to be the chosen people and that South Africa belonged to them. Much earlier, they had begun to work to take control of the government completely instead of sharing control with the English. World War II had come along, and Afrikaners had been divided over whether or not to support the English. These divisions had helped Afrikaner Nationalists, whose political party was the Nationalist Party, consolidate their power. Black Africans were worried about this Afrikaner Nationalist surge, for Afrikaners were traditionally less willing to work with them than the English were.

Black Africans worried in 1936 when the Natives' Trust and Lands Act was passed, fixing the percentage of the country's land available to the Africans at 12.7, leaving over 87 percent for the whites. The Afrikaner Prime Minister, J. B. M. Hertzog, who was responsible for the Act, also passed a series of Segregation Bills that year. These new laws led to greater militancy among young Africans, and at Fort Hare a group of students from the Transkei were particularly incensed. They included a young man from Bizana in Pondoland named Oliver Tambo, and Nelson Mandela, one year younger, who had been born in Qunu near Umtata, the capital of the Transkei "reserve."

Nelson Mandela belonged to the royal family of Thembu. His father, Henry, had been councilor to their relative, the Paramount Chief of Thembu. When Nelson was twelve, his father became ill, and he sent his son to be brought up at the Chief's Great Palace, Mqekezweni. Although the South African government had reduced the status of many chiefs, the Paramount Chief retained certain powers. His wards, which included Nelson, were practically guaranteed a fine education. But Nelson's Xhosa name, Rolihlahla, meant "stirring up trouble," and it proved to be prophetic about his experience at college, especially in a time of black unrest. Unfortunately his career at Fort Hare was cut short when as a member of the Students' Representative Council he participated in a protest after the school authorities reduced the council's powers. He was suspended.

Several years later, in Johannesburg, Tambo and Mandela renewed their friendship, and with a new friend, Walter Sisulu, formed in 1944 a Youth League which became part of the ANC. The basic aims of the League were these: true democracy and full citizenship for Africans, including direct representation in Parliament. Redivision of land among all nationalities in proportion to their numbers. The right of workers to form unions and to strike for better wages and working conditions. Free compulsory education for all children and mass adult education. They wanted to hold strikes and other protests to win more rights, and they fought for five years to get their plan adopted. Finally, in 1949, the ANC agreed to the young people's program of protest and made careful plans to begin it when the time was right. Meanwhile, the ANC had also made alliances with the South African Communist Party, which had been formed in 1921, and with the South African Indian Congress, formed in 1894 by Gandhi, to fight against specific things like the pass laws.

What spurred the moderate, older members of the ANC to agree to the tactics proposed by the younger militants, and what caused the Youth League to agree to the alliance with the Communist Party even though Mandela and Tambo and the others were strongly against Communism, was the election in 1948 of the candidate of the (largely Afrikaner) National Party, D.F. Malan, as Prime Minister. Malan and his party had campaigned on the issue of apartheid, and had beaten out the more moderate Afrikaner and English-speaking candidates. Both militants and moderates in the ANC realized that something had to be done.

In 1950 the government introduced the Population Registration Act, which classified people by race and tribe and which managed to fragment the blacks into so many different ethnic groups that if the Act succeeded, attempts to present a common front would be impaired. On June 26, 1950, the ANC, its Youth League, the Indian Congress, and the Communist Party organized a one-day work stoppage to protest the Act. This protest was successful in some areas, not in others, primarily because the strike had not been well organized nationwide.

Toward the end of that year, Nelson Mandela was elected National President of the Youth League and immediately began to plan for a Defiance Campaign which would start on June 26, 1952, the second anniversary of the one-day strike in 1950. Over the next year and a half he traveled widely to attract support for the campaign, asking for thousands to volunteer in nonviolent protests against apartheid laws.

Mandela and the Youth League did an excellent job in publicizing the upcoming campaign. At Shawbury, the teachers talked about it in excited tones, and transmitted their excitement to the students. Winnie and her schoolmates listened eagerly, and when the Defiance Campaign began, read as much as they could about its progress, mostly in black-run newspapers and magazines.

They were proud to read that more than 8,000 volunteers engaged in the protests, which included entering the "Europeans Only" door at the railroad station in New Brighton township in Port Elizabeth, entering an area without the permits required of nonresidents in the Transvaal, defying the 11 P.M. curfew for blacks in Johannesburg, and leading workers out on strike.

Winnie and her schoolmates read with dismay about how the protestors had been arrested and beaten. They were especially saddened to learn of the arrest of Nelson Mandela, who was their hero, although they had not met him, nor ever expected to do so. While their school was far away from the centers of activity, many of the students felt that they ought to engage in some sort of protest. If there was a Defiance Campaign going on, they ought to "defy," too. They decided to strike against poor school facilities and living conditions.

Winnie understood how the girls felt, but she did not feel she could join in the protest. For one thing, she had been voted chief prefect of the school, with responsibility for all the girls in forms one to five, and was supposed to help maintain student discipline. At Shawbury, there were church services four times a day, the first at 6 A.M., and Winnie helped organize the services. She also led debating clubs. But a far more serious consideration was that she was about to write her matriculation exams. She had not forgotten how much her father and her sister Nancy had sacrificed to send her to a good school, and she could not risk her academic career. She made peace with herself by deciding that at the age of fifteen she had no right to sacrifice all that her loved ones had worked for. She did not join the strike.

Of those who did participate in the protest, many were suspended until the following term, when their reapplications for admission would be accepted. The ringleaders were expelled. Winnie felt guilty about not having joined her schoolmates in the strike, but she put that guilt in the back of her mind as she studied for her examinations. She passed with high marks, which made her eligible for admission to the school of social work in Johannesburg. She was fifteen years old and about to enter yet another part of the larger world that she now knew was out there.

·4·

Johannesburg

*A*fter *passing her examinations at Shawbury, Winnie* returned home to eMbongweni to spend some time with her family. There she met the woman who was soon to be her father's new wife. Hilda Nophikela was a teacher, as Winnie's mother had been, and the whole family liked her and were pleased that Columbus Madikizela was remarrying.

Winnie was especially pleased to see Nancy again, and again she promised her sister that as soon as she was able she would repay her for the sacrifice she had made so that Winnie could go to Shawbury. For her part, Nancy was as proud of Winnie's high pass in the matriculation examinations as she would have been if she herself had gotten the high marks. She was glad to have been able to help out.

Winnie, though only just sixteen, was feeling quite grown up. Already she had been to more places than most Madikizela girls her age, not to mention Madikizela adults. Now she was about to leave for Johannesburg, so far away that it was not even in Transkei, and a real city. In fact, it was the largest city in South Africa. As she looked around her household and her village, she must have realized that things seemed smaller to her now and distances less great. Since very little had changed at home, she saw that it was she who had changed and acquired a different perspective. The larger her world had become, the smaller that little world of her childhood seemed by comparison.

She kept this realization to herself, not wanting to appear brash and overconfident, but her older relatives sensed that she was feeling this way and made a point of giving her advice about how to behave in Johannesburg. While few, if any, of them had ever been to the city, they had heard frightening things about it. Most frightening of all to them were the stories of how rural people had fallen prey to the attractions of city life and forgotten the ways of their rural homes. Winnie's aunts urged her not to forget her heritage, to keep Pondoland and her family close to her heart, and never to do anything in Johannesburg that her family would not approve of.

Winnie certainly did not intend to forsake her heritage. She listened closely and respectfully to what her elders had to say and had no difficulty promising them that she would take their advice. Even before she had heard their warnings, a small part of her had worried about being so far away from home and in such an alien place; now she worried even more.

But her father assured her that he had made arrangements so that she need not feel all alone. He had written letters to the school and learned that Winnie could board at the Helping Hand Hostel in a white, central, part of the city. He had written to the hostel and secured a place for her. He had even arranged for her to travel to Johannesburg in the company of two young male relatives who were going there to work in the nearby gold mines. He had no intention of sending her off on her own to make her way in that alien world, and he assured her that she would be fine. Winnie trusted that he was right.

The train ride to Johannesburg was Winnie's first ever. She did not even mind having to sit in an overcrowded car reserved for blacks, for she was too busy looking out the windows at the countryside as it rushed past her gaze. When the train left Pondoland, she felt a momentary fright, and when she saw the barren, by comparison, terrain around Johannesburg she wondered if she would like the city. Her companions pointed out that it was here that the gold mines were located, and she realized that for all its lush greenness the Transkei did not have any gold.

At the Johannesburg train station, the two men had to leave her in order to meet their contract boss, but Winnie's father had arranged for her to be met. Her "welcoming committee" turned out to be two white women, one of whom was the wife of the man who ran the Jan Hofmeyr School of Social Work. Winnie, who'd had little contact with white people, was relieved to find them friendly and helpful. Later she found out that they were both Americans.

Winnie was awed by Johannesburg. Never before had she seen such tall buildings or so many people. It was hard for her to imagine that so many people existed in the world, let alone in a single city. Less than seventy years earlier, Johannesburg had been nothing but a camp for diggers who came to look for the newly discovered gold.

Nobody knew who "Johannes" was, but he must have been one of the first diggers. He would not have recognized the city that bore his name, with its skyscrapers and office buildings, and its sprawling suburbs, white in one direction, black in the other.

It did not take long for Winnie to discover the real meaning of apartheid in Johannesburg. On the streets of the city all the whites seemed to be well dressed and successful; all the blacks seemed to be servants and beggars. Some of the other girls at the hostel worked as maids for white families, and she learned from them that they were lucky to have such good living conditions; they told her that most black servants had to live in tiny shacks in the backyards of their white employers' homes. But the women who lived at the hostel had their own woes. Few were allowed more than a half day off per week, and for those who had families far away from the city, that meant that they did not get to see their families for months on end. Listening to them, Winnie thought of the young men who had accompanied her on the train from Pondoland to Johannesburg. After they left her at the station, these men signed up for eleven months of work in the mines; they would not see their families during that entire time. They would be allowed to return home for one month before coming back to Johannesburg to sign up for another eleven-month stretch.

The girls at the hostel told Winnie that they were paid poorly, and some worked under employers who treated them badly; but they were afraid to quit their jobs. If they did, the authorities could send them away from Johannesburg for the crime of being unemployed.

After she had been in the city for several months, Winnie visited Soweto, the sprawling black suburb to the southwest of the city (the name Soweto comes from the title South-West Townships). The bus trip she took with some friends was seventeen miles, but only a few miles outside Johannesburg she could see the heavy smog that hung over the cluster of twenty-six townships, where most of the houses were heated and most cooking was done by coal or paraffin fires. More than one million people lived in Soweto, many of them illegally. The row upon row of tiny, identical houses were home to up to twenty people each. There were no paved roads, no streetlights, no electricity. Water came from communal pumps, one tap per block, and since there was no indoor plumbing in most of them, the toilets were outhouses, one serving several families. There were some areas where the houses were of brick, with neat yards surrounded by high fences to keep out thieves, and cars in the driveways; but these "middle-class areas" were few. Most of Soweto was a slum of shacks, deeply rutted streets, rivers of rubbish in the gutters, and a million people who spent most of their time outside because there wasn't room inside. Women cooked on open fires or walked along the alleys, carrying heavy loads on their heads; children played in the garbage-filled empty lots where houses had burned down or been torn down. Unemployed men sat around and talked, or hawked chickens, vegetables, clothing, and whatever else they could sell. Winnie realized that what the people were doing was much the same as people did back in eMbongweni; the difference was their surroundings. Soweto was so depressing compared to the beauty of the Transkei.

Seeing the conditions under which most black people

lived and worked in and around Johannesburg, Winnie came to understand why her family was so bitter against whites, and why the Society of Young Africa and the African National Congress were so popular among blacks. She realized that with all her schoolbook learning, she did not know very much about politics in her own country, and she determined to catch up. In addition to her reading for her courses at the Hofmeyr School of Social Work, she checked out books from the library about African and South African and world history. She wanted to know all she could about how her people had come to such a sorry state, and what could be done about it.

Her classmates at the Hofmeyr School were all very aware politically. They had grown up in urban areas and had greater access to newspapers and magazines than she'd had. Winnie had never before lived in a place where one could get a daily newspaper, and she read the *Golden City Post* as well as other black papers, and the white, English-language *Rand Daily Mail*, which was sympathetic to blacks. She listened to her classmates talk about the latest laws against blacks and the meaning for blacks of various government actions, and she wrote long letters home to her father telling him what she had learned and trying out on him some of her new political opinions. His replies were not encouraging, for he urged her to concentrate on her schoolwork rather than on current events, and implied that politics was not for girls. Winnie was disappointed in her father's attitude. It seemed to her that her female classmates were able to understand politics without losing their femininity. She began to realize that for all his wisdom and learning, there were some things her father had not experienced and did not know. He lived, after all, in an isolated rural area where there were no daily newspapers and no daily contact with whites. When he did have contact with whites, he was always in a powerless position. White school authorities would visit eMbongweni Primary School to see what he was teaching his students. White store clerks in Bizana could refuse to serve him or could assault other blacks without caring how he felt. But at the Hofmeyr School, Winnie was in daily contact with white teachers who were not racist, and who really cared about her education and her development as a human being. Knowing from her own experience that not all whites were enemies of black people, she could not help believing that it might be possible for blacks to win more rights in their own country.

But Winnie did not let her new interest in politics interfere with her studies. She knew that her own future, and her family's finances, depended on her doing well in her first term. School authorities had worried that Winnie, the first rural girl ever accepted at the school, might not be able to adjust to urban life. Because of this worry they had decided not to offer her any sort of scholarship until they were assured that she would continue at the school. For the first six months, her father paid her tuition and fees, and Winnie knew it was a strain on him to do so. She was determined to earn a scholarship so she could relieve him of that burden.

The school authorities had good reason to worry about Winnie. Even though she had an excellent academic record, they were aware that schooling in rural areas like the Transkei was usually inferior to schooling in urban areas. They believed also that young people raised and schooled in rural areas were unprepared to live away from their

families in a world where there were unlimited opportunities to get into trouble. They worried that a young girl
like Winnie might decide she would rather go to the
movies than study, or that she would rather get a job so
she could earn money to buy the dresses in the downtown
stores, or that she would find a boyfriend and decide to
leave school to get married.

During her first six months at the school, Winnie proved
that she was a rural girl who could adjust to urban living
without going astray, that the strict religious orientation of
the school was no more strict than the religious upbring-
ing she had received at home, and that she was capable of
doing the academic work. In fact, she would become the
best student at the school. At the end of the six months,
the school authorities realized they didn't have to worry
about Winnie; they awarded her a full scholarship that
covered all tuition, room and board, and fees.

Even after she had won the scholarship, Winnie continued to study hard. She wanted to get high marks so her
father would be proud of her. And by this time she was
deeply interested in her course work anyway. Seeing the
beggars in Johannesburg and the depressing sights of
Soweto made her believe firmly that one of the best ways
to help her people was to work among them and try to
make their lives better. Lack of education, disease, infant
mortality, malnutrition, unemployment, crime—all these
were problems that blacks in South Africa had in abun-
dance. No population anywhere in the world needed social workers more than they did. Winnie determined to
learn as much as she could about how to reach them, gain
their trust, and help them make their lives better.

In the meantime, however, she was becoming more involved in politics. At first she attended meetings of the Society of Young Africa, now called the Convention, in secret, for students were not supposed to engage in political activity. But as she became friendly with more girls at the hostel, she grew interested in the more activist African National Congress. The majority of the girls were ordinary workers, and they belonged to trade unions as well as to the ANC. Winnie accompanied them to meetings at Trades Hall and read the pamphlets they gave her about the ANC. They talked constantly about the leaders of the ANC—Albert Lutuli, Oliver Tambo, Nelson Mandela, and others—and Winnie came to regard these men as her heroes.

After completion of her course work at the Hofmeyr School, it was time for Winnie to see how to apply what she had learned from books and lectures to a real-life situation. Her course work had already taken her often to Baragwanath Hospital on the outskirts of Soweto, which was the only hospital that served Soweto's blacks. There, she had taught classes in nutrition and health to local people and worked with the doctors and nurses. But the Hofmeyr School required fieldwork in rural areas as well, and Winnie was assigned to do fieldwork at the Ncora-Tsolo Rural Welfare Centre in the Transkei south of Pondoland. It was an area of desperate poverty and high rates of infant death and malnutrition and would be a real test of Winnie's abilities.

Before going to the Centre, Winnie spent a holiday with her family. Now, eMbongweni seemed even smaller to her, and when she thought about how the area to which she was going was even more isolated and rural, she had a brief moment of panic. She had grown to love Johannesburg and urban life, and she worried that she would be homesick for her adopted city. When she saw the reaction of her family and the townspeople when her professor arrived to personally escort her to Tsolo, she worried even more.

Professor Hough, the Field Work Director of the school, was white, and when he and his wife drove into eMbongweni in their shiny car the people of eMbongweni were shocked. They were also suspicious—why would a white man help a black girl? They could not understand that he was concerned about his best pupil and willing to go out of his way to help her.

Once Professor Hough and his wife left her at Tsolo, Winnie felt panicked again. Tsolo was so poverty-stricken and so backward that she wondered what in the world she could do to help the people. She was particularly bothered by the status of women in the area—they acted, and were treated by their husbands, like servants. She realized that things were not much different in eMbongweni, and that her own parents had been unusual because both her mother and her stepmother had been educated. But she also felt that the lowly status of women contributed to the problems at Tsolo. The women, after all, were the ones who cared for the children and prepared the meals. She tried to teach them about hygiene and about the importance of taking advantage of the limited medical facilities that were available to them. She filed numerous reports on conditions in the area in the hope that the government might offer more help. She wondered what all her good grades were worth when she realized how little she could do. But she also realized that she had to stick it out, and though she missed Johannesburg and her friends, she was determined to stay on until her assigned period of field-work ended.

But one day as Winnie filled out papers in her office at the Ncora-Tsolo Rural Welfare Centre, an old woman from Bizana came in and asked her if she was pleased about the marriage her father had arranged for her. This was news to Winnie. What marriage? To whom? The woman told her that her father had arranged for her to marry the son of a respected chief in the Transkei. At present, the son was attending Lovedale College. Winnie had heard of Chief Quaquani, but she had never met either him or his son. She was expected to marry a stranger.

Arranged marriages were customary among the Pondo. Usually, elders discussed who among the young would marry each other. They would inform the fathers of their decisions, and the fathers then informed their sons and daughters. The process was not new to Winnie. What was new, and shocking, was that it applied to her. She did not believe that her father had originated the idea. After all, he had chosen his two wives himself. But she also realized that he was likely to obey the elders. And she, in turn, was supposed to obey her father.

But she could not. She could not even think of marriage. She'd never even had a real boyfriend. At school, her classmates had sometimes teased her about that, for Winnie was a beautiful girl who could have had her pick of boyfriends. But Winnie had always been more intent on studying and doing well in school than dating and having boyfriends. And she had never met a boy who came up to her standards, which were based mostly on her father and on her male teachers at the Hofmeyr School.

Even if she had met a boy she liked, she had other goals

in life. She wanted to get her degree in medical social work. She wanted to have a career. Eventually she wanted to get married and have children, but she was only nineteen and had plenty of time. No, marriage was not for her now, and especially not to a stranger. She could just imagine getting married to a strange man and going off to live in some rural area of the Transkei and having babies and never seeing Johannesburg again. That was not what she wanted out of life.

But how could she disobey her father? A Pondo girl simply did not do that. She realized that it would be useless to try to talk to her father about it; no matter what he thought privately, he would be pressed to go along with tradition and with the decision of the elders. He would be forced to insist that she obey. In fact, Winnie realized, if she stayed in the Transkei she would be pressured from all directions. All the people she was trying to help would expect her to obey, and if she resisted they would turn away from her.

At length Winnie decided that she had to leave the Transkei, even though that meant giving up her fieldwork before it was completed. Once she had made her decision, she wasted no time in acting upon it. She apologized to her supervisor but explained that she could not stay at the Centre, packed her bags, and beat a hasty retreat to Johannesburg.

From the safety of the city she had come to love, she wrote to her father to explain that she could not agree to an arranged marriage and hoped he would understand. She was also able to tell him that not only had she passed her matriculation examination but had won a prize as best student. Soon afterward she was also able to report that she had been offered a full scholarship to study in the United States.

America was a magic name to Winnie, as it was to her friends and schoolmates. They eagerly read newspaper articles about the United States and imagined that it was a rich land full of wonderful music and stylish people and exciting movies. They were dimly aware that there was racial segregation in America, but that it was not as severe as apartheid. They had also read that black people in America were beginning to demonstrate for more rights. Just a year or so before Winnie won her degree, black people in a place called Montgomery, Alabama, had boycotted the city buses in protest over laws under which blacks had to sit in the back of the buses and even give up their seats there to whites if a bus became crowded. After over a year of staying off the buses, the boycotters had won a decision by the U.S. Supreme Court outlawing this segregation.

Winnie realized that she was very lucky to be offered an opportunity to study in America, and part of her wanted to go. But part of her did not want to leave Johannesburg and her friends, not to mention her family and her country. She could not seem to make up her mind, and she sent a telegram to her father, asking his advice. He replied that the decision was hers to make, which did not help her at all.

Meanwhile, because she was no longer a student, Winnie had moved to a different area of the Helping Hand Hostel, where working women lived. Her bed was right next to that of Adelaide Tsukudu, a nurse at Baragwanath Hospital, and the two soon became good friends. Adelaide talked often about her work, and Winnie was extremely interested. She was also interested to learn that Adelaide was dating Oliver Tambo, a black lawyer in Johannesburg who was a leader in the African National Congress. With a partner, Tambo had set up the first black law practice in central Johannesburg. Tambo's partner in his law practice was none other than Nelson Mandela, the ANC leader who had become a hero to Winnie while she was at Shawbury and following the Defiance Campaign that the ANC staged during 1951–1952. Adelaide knew all about the activities of the ANC, and Winnie was fascinated to hear her talk about them.

Since Winnie's newest close friend worked at Baragwanath Hospital, she was struck by the great coincidence when out of the blue, she received a letter from the hospital offering her a job as the first black medical social worker in South Africa. But when she got over her first excitement at receiving the letter, Winnie realized she was in an even greater quandary than she had been before. She had been offered two wonderful opportunities, but she could choose only one. *And*, she had to make the decision herself. No one, not her father, nor her professors, nor her best friends, could advise her.

Winnie thought and thought, and at length she chose not to go to America. She decided that she could make a greater contribution as the first black medical social worker in the history of South Africa. If she did well, then she might open doors for others. And there was no question that her people needed her. She decided that they should come first.

· 5 ·
Nelson Mandela

*W*innie's arrival at *Baragwanath Hospital was cele*-brated in the Johannesburg black press. Photographers took her picture and reporters interviewed her about her early life. Not only was she the first black medical social worker in the country, she was also a girl from rural Pondoland who had succeeded against many odds. She was delighted with all the attention and sent clippings from the newspapers to her father, hoping that they would help him believe she had made the right choice in not agreeing to an arranged marriage. The attention also helped her to believe that she had made the right choice in accepting the position at Baragwanath and turning down the scholarship to America. Later, she would become more and more certain that her choice had been the correct one, for if she had not accepted the post at the hospital there would not have been even one black medical social worker in all of South Africa.

Two years earlier, in 1954, the government had passed the Bantu Education Act, one of many laws designed to segregate Africans into various homelands based on tribal divisions. The term Bantu refers primarily to a group of languages, including Swahili, Zulu, and Kafir, and under the Bantu Education law, black children were supposed to acquire a solid foundation in tribal life, which would prepare them for a productive future in their respective homelands. Hendrik Verwoerd, the Minister for Native Affairs who would become Prime Minister in 1958, explained that teaching a black child the same subjects as whites was "misleading him by showing him the green pastures of European society, in which he is not allowed to graze. Bantu Education should not be used to create imitation whites." They should not be taught history and math, but gardening and tree planting, woodworking and sewing, so as to prepare them for the menial jobs they were expected to take. They also should not be taught in English but only in Afrikaans and their native languages. Not long after Winnie graduated from the Hofmeyr School of Social Work, the government closed the school down. From then on, blacks who wished to study social work had to attend the new "bush colleges" that the government was setting up in the homelands.

The black doctors and nurses at Baragwanath Hospital, all of whom had, like Winnie, been educated under the old laws, were furious over the Bantu Education Act. They were also angry that they were paid less than the white doctors at the hospital. During Winnie's first few months there, the black doctors went out on strike in protest over this unequal treatment, but they were unable to win any concessions from the hospital authorities.

In those first few months, Winnie was far more concerned with learning her duties and doing well at her job than with the politics at the hospital. From the start, she impressed her co-workers with her hard work and willingness to do even more than was expected of her. While walking in the streets she kept a sharp eye out for the destitute, and would persuade those who needed medical treatment to come to the hospital. Part of her job was to write to employers to explain why their workers needed a leave of absence for an operation. She could be very convincing and firm with bosses who were angry about losing their laborers for any reason.

A major part of her job was working with new mothers and their babies. After they left the hospital, she visited their homes in order to show them how to care for the infants, for many did not know about proper hygiene and feeding. She now visited Soweto regularly and saw what went on behind the walls of the little houses. What she saw often caused her to despair, for the houses were overcrowded and poorly furnished and their inhabitants clearly unable to afford proper food for themselves or for their children. Yet she usually found the people trying hard and doing the best they could under horrible conditions.

Those who did not try were a problem. Sometimes mothers abandoned their newborn infants at the hospital, and it was Winnie's job to search for the mothers. It was also her job to find relatives of patients who died in the hospital. She was remarkably successful after she came up with the idea of working with the black *Golden City Post*. The paper would announce the names of people she was searching for, and often this would help her to find them. She also talked the paper into helping her raise money to pay for funerals for people who died without leaving any relatives. She was pleased with her success and felt that she had really found her true calling in social work.

Not long after she started work at the hospital, Winnie met Chief Kaiser Matanzima, who visited with a group of important people from the Transkei. Matanzima, though he was the nephew of Nelson Mandela, had very different ideas about what was possible for blacks in South Africa. He was prepared to go along with the government's plans for homelands, even though that meant depriving the people in those homelands of their South African citizenship. He was also prepared to be President of the new Transkei state when it was officially created. He wanted to visit Baragwanath Hospital because he wanted eventually to establish a similar hospital in the Transkei.

When he met Winnie, he forgot about hospitals and concentrated on social work. He asked her all sorts of questions about her work and suggested that she should return with him to the Transkei and run the Ncora-Tsolo Welfare Centre, where she had done her fieldwork for her degree at the Hofmeyr School. He invited her to dinner to discuss the matter. That evening, a car picked her up at the hostel and drove her to a house in Orlando West, one of the Soweto townships, where Chief Matanzima was waiting with an elaborate dinner and equally elaborate plans for the two of them. Winnie did not wish to be impolite to the thirty-nine-year-old chief, and she was flattered by his attentions, but she had no wish to return to the Transkei.

After Matanzima returned home, he wrote to Winnie frequently, and she answered each letter out of politeness. But when she learned that he had instructed his representatives to negotiate with her father to marry her, she stopped answering his letters. She did not agree with his politics, thought he was too old, and besides, she did not love him. She intended to marry for love.

Winnie continued to live at the Helping Hand Hostel. Not only had it become "home" to her, it was relatively inexpensive, and that was important to Winnie. She tried to send as much of her salary back home to her family as she could, and one of her first goals was to repay her older sister, Nancy, for her sacrifice. Years earlier, Nancy had quit school so that the money that was being spent on her schooling could be used for Winnie's. Now, Winnie sent home money to enable Nancy to come to Johannesburg, and she arranged for Nancy to train as a nurse's aide at the Bridgeman Memorial Hospital in the city.

Adelaide was still Winnie's closest friend at the hostel, though Winnie suspected that it would not be too long before Adelaide married Oliver Tambo and moved out. At length, Winnie got a chance to meet Tambo, and was surprised and delighted to learn that she was his niece. In the complicated relationships of her huge, extended family, there were many, many relatives she had never met. Oliver had grown up in Bizana but was seventeen years older than Winnie, and so when as a child Winnie had attended celebrations of the extended family, Oliver was already away at boarding school or at Fort Hare University.

Not long after that, Winnie met Nelson Mandela. It was not the first time she had ever seen him. She had seen him once before when she had gone to Johannesburg Regional Court for the trial of a co-worker who had been assaulted by the police. Nelson Mandela represented the co-worker, and Winnie found the lawyer and veteran freedom-fighter towering and imposing. As he walked into court, the crowd whispered his name, and she felt that she was in the presence of someone very special. Thus, when she actually met him, she was awe-struck, not only because he was a living legend but also because of the sheer physical presence of the man. He was tall, 6 feet 3 inches, and powerfully built, and he had about him an air of confidence that seemed to charge the atmosphere around him with a special kind of electricity.

It was a chance meeting. She had just gotten off the bus from Baragwanath Hospital when Oliver Tambo and Winnie's friend Adelaide Tsukudu drove by and offered her a lift back to the hostel. On the way Adelaide asked Oliver to stop at a delicatessen. He stopped, then realized he had no money. But then he saw that his partner, Nelson Mandela, was in the shop. "Tell him to pay," said Tambo. Adelaide went into the delicatessen, and a few minutes later came out with Mandela. Tambo introduced Winnie as "Winnie from Bizana."

Winnie was so in awe of the man that she was tongue-tied and afterward could barely remember even what he had said to her. She did not think she had made much of an impression on him. But clearly she had, for soon afterward he called her at the hospital and invited her to lunch that weekend. He said he wanted to discuss raising money, and Winnie agreed, though she wondered how in the world she could help since she had never done any fund-raising except to pay for the funerals of patients who had died in the hospital.

It was a Sunday, and Nelson sent a car to pick up Winnie at the hostel and take her to his office. Winnie had tried on every dress she owned and not been satisfied;

finally she had borrowed a dress that made her look at least a bit older and more sophisticated. But she wondered if Nelson even noticed. There were all sorts of people at the office, wanting to talk to Nelson. He barely had a chance to give her a smile in between consultations.

At last he excused himself and took her by the arm and said it was time for lunch. Nelson took her to an Indian restaurant and ordered a curried dish, and it was so spicy that tears ran down her cheeks. She could barely finish her meal and wondered what he must think of her. She also felt very left out. During the entire meal, they were constantly interrupted by people wanting to talk with Nelson. When they left the restaurant, they were stopped every couple of steps. "Nelson couldn't walk from here to there without having consultations," she said later. Finally they drove out of town where they walked in the veld and finally had a chance to talk.

Nelson did discuss the need to raise money for the Treason Trial Fund, and Winnie quickly got over her shyness as she listened to his story. The need for funds was a grave one. The previous year, 1956, the police had arrested nearly all the leaders of the ANC as well as a number of minor organizers (a total of 156 men and women) and charged them with high treason. The government's case against these people was based on the belief that the liberation movement was part of an international Communist-inspired effort to overthrow the government by violence. The ANC and the arrested men and women themselves had used up most of their money just paying the bail bonds so they could get out of prison while they waited for their trial. Now they had to raise money to pay their legal fees and to help the families of those men who had lost their jobs when they were arrested. This was difficult to do because Nelson and all the others were "banned persons."

The concept of banning in South Africa dates back to the Suppression of Communism Act that was passed in 1950. This act had contained a page or two of restrictions against people suspected of being Communists—restrictions like not attending meetings of leftist organizations and not publishing "Communist" pamphlets. Since these restrictions could be imposed on anyone without formally charging them or producing any evidence against them, they proved to be a handy tool for the government. In fact, they were so handy that over the years the government kept adding on more banning orders, more restrictions on people's activities. Banning orders the government could impose under the Suppression of Communism Act eventually grew from one or two pages to eight or ten pages. A banned person like Nelson Mandela led a severely restricted life, and Winnie wondered how he could seem so confident with so much against him and the threat of reimprisonment looming before him, not to mention the actual trial itself, whenever it took place.

Nelson asked Winnie about her early life and told her about his own. While she already knew a lot about him from newspaper and magazine articles, Winnie listened in rapt attention, for she was fascinated by this man. Although, at thirty-six, he was much younger than her father, there were things about him that reminded her of the older man. He was certainly the most articulate man she had ever heard, next to her father. By comparison, she felt very uneducated and unsophisticated, and was especially embarrassed that she knew nothing about Indian food. As they walked along the rocky path to the car, Winnie slipped and broke the strap of her sandal. Nelson took her hand and guided her, barefoot, to the car. Just before they got into the car he turned to her and said, "It was a lovely day," and kissed her.

The next day, Nelson visited her at the hospital. Again, he talked at first about raising money for the Treason Trial Fund, but pretty soon they were discussing other things. And so it went for several weeks. Winnie knew she was enjoying the attention, but she was not sure how she felt about their relationship. She addressed him as Chief Mandela, out of respect for his hereditary position, and told herself that he was only interested in her as a fund-raiser. She didn't even tell her best friend Adelaide that they were seeing each other.

But she often found herself thinking about what it would be like to marry this man. She forced herself to eat the Indian food he liked so much, and when they visited Indian friends of his she asked the women to show her how to prepare their special recipes. She sometimes found herself wondering what her father would think of Nelson Mandela, and worrying about the reasons her father would disapprove of him, at least as a husband for his daughter.

Mandela was sixteen years older than she was, for one thing. Far more serious was the fact that he was separated from his wife and soon to be divorced. As a young man, he, like Winnie, had run away rather than accept an arranged marriage. He had gone to Johannesburg, gotten a job in a law office, and started taking law courses at the University of Witwatersrand (Ridge of White Waters). He had met a nurse named Evelyn Ntoko Mase at the City

Deep Mine Hospital and married her. They had moved
into a house in the township of Orlando and had three
children, two boys and a girl. They'd had a good marriage
at first, and Nelson loved his children, but his deepening
involvement in political activity had kept him away often.
By 1955, the pressures and the dangers of his political life
had strongly affected the marriage. He and Evelyn had
separated, and after a time were divorced.

In the course of their various discussions, Nelson made
it very clear to Winnie that his life was devoted to the
struggle for his people. In fact, she took his intensity on
the subject as a sign that he was not planning to get married again and that he really was only interested in her for
how she could help him politically. She could not blame
him for not wanting the responsibility of a wife, for he had
no way of knowing how long it would be before he was
convicted of high treason and imprisoned.

But he kept calling and visiting and asking her to dinner, and she kept meeting him and wondering where it
would all lead. As the weeks went by she came to understand that in his own way he was making as much time as
he could to be with her. He would send his car to pick her
up and take her to a nearby gymnasium, where he would
talk with her while he worked out. He would stop by in
his car and talk with her for a few moments before he
dashed off to a meeting. Winnie later recalled, "Even at
that stage, life with him was life without him. He did not
even pretend that I would have some special claim to his
time."

Then, Chief Kaiser Matanzima arrived in town. He had
returned from the Transkei to find out why Winnie had
stopped answering his letters. He called her at the hospi-

tal and told her that a car would pick her up after work and take her to the same house in Orlando West where they had had dinner together before. Winnie was too surprised to respond, and the chief took it for granted that she would come. That evening, still dressed in her white hospital uniform, Winnie was driven to the house, and was shocked when the door opened and there stood not only Chief Kaiser Matanzima but also Chief Nelson Mandela. Mandela was Matanzima's uncle, and both the house and the car belonged to Mandela!

The two men were as surprised as Winnie. They looked at each other, then at her, and in an instant both realized that they were pursuing the same woman. They could not talk about it then, for other men were at the house for a political meeting. They gave each other, and Winnie, hard looks, and then joined the other men. Winnie was expected to wait until the meeting was over.

Winnie did not wait. She fled the house. She did not know how she had managed to get involved in such a sticky situation, but she did know that she could not handle it right then. She beat a hasty retreat to the hostel and after calming down, decided that it was up to the two men to work the problem out between them. She hoped that Nelson Mandela would win out, but she wasn't even sure he cared enough to do so.

It was a tense time for the two men, but eventually Chief Kaiser Matanzima bowed to his uncle and stopped pursuing Winnie. As for Nelson Mandela, the incident spurred him to declare his feelings for Winnie. Not long afterward he and Winnie were driving in his car. Suddenly Nelson pulled over to the side of the road and stopped. He turned to Winnie and said, "You know, there is a woman, a dressmaker, you must go and see her, she is going to make your wedding gown. How many bridesmaids would you like to have?'' *That* was the way he proposed marriage to Winnie! Only then did she realize that his divorce from his first wife, Evelyn, had become final and that he considered himself free to marry again. (Thembu tradition made it possible for Nelson to have more than one wife, but he did not believe in that custom.)

It was not a romantic proposal, but Winnie understood that Nelson had too much on his mind to be romantic. He was a 'banned person who would soon go to trial and might be convicted and imprisoned for a long time. Even if by some miracle he was acquitted, he would still not be able to be the kind of husband she deserved—one who always came home at night and who concentrated all his attention on her and the children he would like to have with her. But Winnie didn't care what she would have to go through, she wanted to be with him.

Winnie was, however, worried about what her father would think. Both she and Nelson felt that they must bow to tradition and seek her father's consent. Ordinarily, Nelson should have traveled to Pondoland to ask Columbus Madikizela for his consent, but the banning orders against Nelson prevented him from leaving Johannesburg. So Winnie had to go. As she had feared, her father was greatly against the marriage. But Winnie's stepmother took her side, and by this time Columbus Madikizela had pretty much accepted the fact that Winnie was going to do what she wanted to do. He could not help regretting, however, that she had turned down marriages to a chief and a chief's son and now wanted to marry a divorced chief who would most likely be going to prison shortly.

By the time Winnie visited her father, the date for the beginning of the Treason Trial had been set for the first of August 1958. Winnie and Nelson discussed the possibility of delaying their marriage until the trial was over and Nelson's fate was known, but they decided not to. They wanted to be married when the trial began.

Preparations for their marriage were a curious blend of traditional and very modern practices. Nelson's representatives negotiated Winnie's "bride price" with her father and agreed to pay Columbus Madikizela a certain number of cattle (the bride is not to know how many cattle are paid for her, and Winnie still does not know). Winnie insisted on being married in her home and Winnie's parents got word to the hundreds of relatives who had to be invited to such an important event. When her parents realized just how many guests there would be, they took an unusual step. They asked to hire the Bizana Town Hall for the wedding reception. No black event had ever been held there, but surprisingly the authorities consented. Meanwhile authorities in Johannesburg granted Nelson the right to leave the district for four days to attend his own wedding.

Completely nontraditional was the prenuptial contract that Nelson and Winnie signed. This was an agreement, signed before their marriage, that gave Winnie control over the possessions that she brought to the marriage. Traditionally, once a woman married a man, the man came to control the possessions of both, and the woman had few rights. Nelson believed that women should have more rights, and besides, he wanted to make sure her property was legally protected in case he was sent to prison.

By tradition, a father always spoke certain "words of

wisdom" to his daughter before the wedding. Columbus Madikizela wondered what kind of advice he could possibly give to this headstrong girl, not yet twenty-three, who had cast her lot with a much older, divorced man who had made it clear that his political activities came first. Finally Columbus Madikizela told Winnie simply that she was marrying the struggle, not the man. Winnie was caught up in the excitement of her wedding plans and preparations; she wasn't thinking a whole lot about politics. But she had already accepted what her father was saying as fact. As she said later, "One became so much part and parcel of Nelson if you knew him that you automatically expected anything that happened to him to happen to yourself, and it didn't really matter. He gave you such confidence, such faith and courage. If you became involved in our cause as he was, it was just not possible to think in terms of yourself at all."

The wedding took place at the Bizana Methodist Church on June 14, 1958. Winnie wore a Western-style gown—white satin and lace with a veil. The reception at the Bizana Town Hall was also Western-style, for the benefit of the many friends from Johannesburg who had traveled to Bizana to attend the wedding. When it was over, all the hundreds of local relatives went to eMbongweni for the traditional reception, a week of feasting and dancing that the bride and groom could share for only a couple of days. Nelson could be away from Johannesburg for only four days, and they had to get back to the city before the celebrations were over. For this reason, too, the couple was unable to observe the tradition that the wedding ceremony should take place in both their homes. Nelson's home village of Qunu was too far away for them to be able to travel there and still get back to Johannesburg on time. According to Winnie, "As far as the elders in my family are concerned, we haven't finished getting married to this day." Winnie kept part of the wedding cake so that one day they would be able to complete their marriage by cutting it at Nelson's home. She still has that part of her wedding cake.

Nelson and Winnie Mandela on their
wedding day, June 14, 1958. • *Eli Weinberg, I.D.A.F.*

Nelson Mandela, 1961. ▪ *Wide World Photos.*

Winnie with Zindzi and Zeni, 1961. • I.D.A.F.

Winnie in traditional dress entering the court
in Pretoria where Nelson was on trial, 1962. ▪ *Wide World Photos.*

Winnie escorts Nelson's mother through a police
cordon outside the court in Pretoria, 1964. ▪ *Wide World Photos.*

Winnie in traditional Xhosa dress, 1978. ▪ *I.D.A.F.*

Winnie receives the Robert F. Kennedy Memorial Human Rights Award from John Buchanan at a hotel outside Johannesburg, 1986. ▪ *Wide World Photos*.

Winnie arrives at Pollsmoor Maximum Security Prison, where Nelson is held, with Dr. Allan Boesak, 1986. ▪ *Habans/Sygma.*

Winnie helps distribute food aid from the West German
embassy to the poor in Brandfort, 1986. ▪ *Wide World Photos.*

Winnie with Coretta Scott King at her home in Soweto, 1986. ▪ *Durand/Sygma.*

Zindzi, younger daughter of Winnie and Nelson, 1986.
▪ *Mohamed Lounes/Gamma.*

·6·

Life With Nelson Mandela

*B*ack in Johannesburg, Winnie moved into Nelson's house at 8115 Orlando (his ex-wife and their three children lived elsewhere in Johannesburg). While it was small—with a kitchen, a bedroom, and a front room—it was much nicer than most houses in Soweto. It had running water, hot water, electricity, and an indoor bathroom. Nelson told Winnie that he had been allowed to choose it when the houses in that area were being built in the 1940s. At the time, he was working for the Orlando City Council, and the superintendent of the council invited him to choose for himself one of the new houses. Nelson could have chosen a four-room house, but he did not feel he should take advantage of the superintendent's generosity, so he chose the smallest house. Winnie later said that it was typical of Nelson to do that: "He must have the last of everything in life."

Winnie supervised the addition of two rooms and redecorated the inside. Outside, she planted a small garden. She wanted the house to be a place that Nelson would want to come home to as often as possible, and in the first weeks of their marriage he did try to spend as much time as he could at home with her. But there were usually other people around, just as there were usually other people around Nelson at his office and wherever else he went. Often, Nelson would arrive home with several people in tow and announce to Winnie that he had brought them home for dinner. Winnie, having prepared a nice dinner for two, would tearfully explain that there wasn't enough food, but he would just laugh and go to a nearby store for more. On weekends, Nelson's three children sometimes visited, and there were few moments when the newlyweds actually were alone. Even when they were alone, they were not safe from rude interruptions.

Not long after their marriage, she and Nelson were awakened in the middle of the night by police banging on their door. The security police had arrived to conduct a search for incriminating papers. Winnie watched in horror as they pulled books from the shelves, scattered the contents of drawers, and generally made a mess, all the while talking about Kaffirs. They found nothing, and once Winnie got over her fright, she was furious. But Nelson told her she might as well get used to such raids, for the authorities would not stop until they had found a way to put him in jail.

Meanwhile, Nelson prepared for his trial, which began on August 1, 1958. This Treason Trial, as it came to be known, was held in Pretoria, forty miles from Johannesburg, and he stayed in Pretoria most of the time because it was too far to commute. Of the 156 people arrested in 1956, 152 remained charged, and with so many defendants the trial promised to be a long one. It was also very well attended. The case had attracted worldwide attention, and there were many foreign observers in the courtroom. Perhaps fearful that world opinion would be automatically against a trial with so many defendants, the government dropped its charges against sixty-one of them, including Albert Lutuli and Oliver Tambo. Along with Walter Sisulu, Nelson was among the ninety-one people now formally charged with high treason.

Winnie sometimes attended the trial with her husband, but he suggested that she would be more helpful working in the struggle. Besides, she was still working at Baragwanath Hospital and knew that her job was crucial, for Nelson was not working and her salary was all they had to live on. In her capacity as a social worker, however, she could still help the struggle. She visited the families of the defendants and tried to help those who had no income while their husbands and fathers were on trial.

She joined the ANC Women's League and attended classes where she learned how to make public speeches. The women would write out speeches and then deliver them to others in the league, and the audiences would criticize them. After a time, Winnie came to feel capable of delivering public speeches, but she didn't get a chance to share her pride with her husband; there just wasn't time to talk about such minor things. She even stopped worrying that he might get a chance to come home and not find her there. She went to her nighttime meetings, and tried not to feel guilty on the rare occasions when she found that he had indeed come home to find her gone. She realized that she would just have to do what she felt was right and hope that she made the right decisions.

One major decision she had to make herself during the

early months of her marriage was whether or not to demonstrate against the government's new pass laws for black women. In 1958, Hendrik Verwoerd was elected Prime Minister of South Africa, and he wasted no time pursuing the policies aimed at segregating blacks into homelands that he had started as Minister for Native Affairs. Previously, only black men had been required to carry passes; now a law was proposed that required them also of black women.

The Women's Federation of the African National Congress organized demonstrations against the new pass law. Winnie wanted to take part, but she was certain that if she were arrested she would lose her job at Baragwanath Hospital. Also, she was pregnant by this time, and she knew enough about how the police treated prisoners to realize that if she joined the demonstrations she would be putting not just her own life at stake but that of her unborn child. But she chose to demonstrate anyway. And when Nelson came home one day in October 1958, Winnie was not there, for she had been arrested.

More than one thousand women, some carrying their babies, were crowded first into police vans and then into cold stone cells with only thin straw mats on the floors. Each woman was given a filthy blanket that smelled of urine. It was Winnie's first time in prison, and she was frightened. When she began to bleed, she was terrified that she was about to have a miscarriage and lose her child. Fortunately, Albertina Sisulu, wife of ANC President Walter Sisulu, was in the cell with her; she wrapped Winnie in her own overcoat and fed her some of the prison food. Winnie stopped bleeding and did not lose the baby. But two weeks in prison hardly contributed to her good health.

When she was released, she was overjoyed to find her husband waiting for her, but he soon had to leave again, and she had to face alone her dismissal from Baragwanath Hospital. She was not surprised at losing her job for demonstrating against the pass laws for women, but she was worried that there would not be enough money to live on. With a baby on the way, they needed money. Fortunately, she was offered another job almost immediately, and while she regretted having to leave the job she had enjoyed at Baragwanath Hospital, she came to like her new position with the Johannesburg Child Welfare Society.

In January 1959, sixty-one of the Treason Trial defendants were released when their indictments were quashed. This left thirty defendants, including Nelson Mandela and Walter Sisulu, of the 156 people originally arrested in 1956. Even those remaining were delighted, however, for it seemed to them proof that the government did not have a strong case. But the government continued to pursue the case against the remaining thirty.

During a recess in the trial, Nelson returned home briefly before leaving for an out-of-town ANC meeting. Winnie was due to have her baby shortly, and Nelson assured her that he would be back in time. But Winnie went into labor earlier than expected, and though there were plenty of friends around to take her to Baragwanath Hospital and visit her there, the one person she wanted most in the world to be with her was her husband, and he missed the birth of their first child, a girl whom they named Zenani and called Zeni. Winnie was furious, and

Nelson knew she would be. When he visited her in the hospital he brought along a friend, knowing that Winnie would not berate him in front of other people.

Once she had recuperated, Winnie went back to work at the Child Welfare Society and rejoined her husband in the struggle, putting aside whatever lingering resentment she felt over his absence when Zeni was born. He had a lot on his mind. Not only did he have to worry about the Treason Trial, but there was much unrest among blacks over the new pass laws and the ANC was having trouble channeling it into effective protest.

In many parts of the country, activist blacks were beginning to feel that the day for nonviolent protest had passed. One reason why they felt this way was that world opinion seemed to be coming down more and more on the side of African independence. At the United Nations, the year 1960 was proclaimed Africa Year to celebrate international acceptance of the principle of African independence after many years of colonialism. In 1960 alone, independence was granted to the former French colonies of Cameroon, the Central African Republic, Chad, Republic of the Congo-Brazzaville, Dahomey, Gabon, Ivory Coast, the Malagasy Republic, Mali, Mauritania, Niger, Senegal, and Upper Volta. Also in 1960 the Republic of the Congo (later renamed Zaire), Nigeria, Somali Democratic Republic, and Togo became independent. The independence of other African countries was scheduled by the Portuguese and the British in the coming years. But in South Africa the only change in the works was to make the Union of South Africa the Republic of South Africa in 1961. This separation from the British Empire and change in the form of government would have absolutely no effect on the status of blacks and whites in the country. Many politicized blacks in South Africa wanted to know why.

By this time, even blacks in the remote rural areas had become politicized. In Pondoland, Winnie's home area of the Transkei, the government had been taking steps to establish another Bantu homeland, and her own father had become embroiled in the controversy. He supported the government, much to Winnie's dismay, and though she could not agree with him she still felt a terrible sense of divided loyalty when leaders of the Pondoland resistance secretly visited Nelson to ask him how to proceed. She felt even worse when the conflict in Pondoland resulted in a minor civil war, and her father, who would be named Minister of Lands and Agriculture of the new Transkei Homeland, was attacked as a collaborator. Much later she said, "To see the anger, to see and feel the anger of the people my father in his own twisted way had tried to sacrifice so much for. It was tragic that politically my father and I did not see eye to eye. It left terrible scars in my heart." Meanwhile, Nelson Mandela, too, was suffering divided political loyalties, for his nephew, Kaiser Matanzima, had continued to cooperate with the government and would become Prime Minister of the new Transkei "homeland."

Unrest in the ANC also led to a rift within that organization in 1959, when Robert Sobukwe, a graduate of Fort Hare University who had become a lecturer at the University of Witwatersrand, led a breakaway faction in the founding of a new organization, the Pan Africanist Congress (PAC). The slogan of the new organization was Independence in 1963.

The ANC leaders realized that they had to be even more

activist in order to keep the allegiance of their remaining members, and they planned a new round of demonstrations to begin on March 31, 1960. But ten days before that, the PAC launched its own series of protests against the pass laws. At the brand-new township of Sharpeville outside Vereeniging in the southern Transvaal, members of PAC marched peacefully to the police station without their passes and were almost immediately fired upon by seventy-five policemen, who considered the crowd "menacing." More than 700 shots blasted at the crowd, and 69 blacks were killed, another 180 wounded. The PAC, the ANC, and the international press called it a massacre. The same day, another demonstration was put down in Langa, outside Cape Town, and two were killed, forty-nine injured.

A new wave of strikes and demonstrations followed, and the government soon declared a state of emergency. Under it, the authorities immediately imprisoned Nelson Mandela, Albert Lutuli, and the twenty-nine other defendants in the Treason Trial. The government also outlawed the ANC and the PAC, declaring them unlawful organizations. Fortunately, Oliver Tambo was out of the country at the time; he would keep the ANC alive by setting up offices in Britain and Tanzania.

Meanwhile, at the Treason Trial, the team of defense lawyers walked out, protesting that it was impossible to represent the defendants under the state of emergency. In the absence of their attorneys, the defendants agreed that Nelson Mandela and Duma Nokwe, his friend, should take over their defense. In early August 1960, Nelson arose in court to present his evidence and to be cross-examined. Winnie had traveled to Johannesburg to see him testify. Along with the many representatives of the international press, she marveled at his composure and at his ability to articulate his beliefs and those of the ANC under the badgering questions of the prosecutors.

Most of the questions from the prosecution centered on speeches he had made and articles he had written. From time to time, one of the three judges asked him a question. One day a judge asked, "Isn't your freedom a direct threat to the Europeans?" [He meant the white South Africans.] Mandela answered, "We are not antiwhite, we are against white supremacy, and in struggling against white supremacy, we have the support of some sections of the European population. . . . It is quite clear that the ANC has consistently preached a policy of racial harmony and we have condemned racialism no matter by whom it is professed."

At the end of August, the state of emergency was at last lifted and for the first time in five months Nelson was able to return home to Winnie and Zeni. But from the moment he walked in the door, the telephone started to ring and people arrived to see him. Winnie was pregnant again and would like to have had some time alone with her husband, but she did not complain. She was so pleased to have him home that the only nagging she allowed herself was about his poor eating habits—he did not even give himself time for proper meals.

Soon he had to return to Pretoria for the resumption of the Treason Trial, although at least now he would not have the responsibility of conducting the defense himself. With the lifting of the state of emergency, the original defense team agreed to return. The trial had now been going on for two years, and there was no telling how much longer it would last.

The court adjourned the trial for the Christmas holidays, and Nelson went home. Winnie was due to deliver their second child that month, and she thought that her husband would be with her this time. But then Nelson's family in the Transkei sent word that his younger son, Makgatho, who had been staying with them, was ill. Nelson was still under banning orders and was not supposed to leave Johannesburg, but he defied the bans to drive to the Transkei to get his son and bring him back to Johannesburg for medical care. In his absence, Winnie gave birth to their second daughter, Zindziswa, whom they called Zindzi. It was a difficult birth, and while the baby was fine, Winnie was very ill. Nelson returned to Johannesburg only to find that he had missed the birth of their second child and that Winnie was not doing at all well. He rushed to Bridgeman Memorial Hospital, where he found that Winnie was being cared for in the nonwhite section, which automatically meant she was not getting the same care as a white woman in the same condition. Furious, Nelson picked up his wife and child and took them home. From there he called the family doctor who had attended Winnie during the birth of Zeni, and she soon recovered.

Well again, Winnie returned to work at the Child Welfare Center. Friends took care of Zeni and Zindzi each day. Winnie would have liked the opportunity to stay at home with them, but she was still the major breadwinner of the family—someone had to keep a roof over their heads and food in their stomachs. By this time, the Treason Trial was in its third year. The defendants and their supporters did not feel that the government had presented a strong enough case to convict them; but the prosecutors seemed to have decided that if they dragged the trial on long enough they could win by the sheer volume of their testimony. Then one day in the middle of March one of the judges suddenly called a week's recess. No one knew why. At the end of the recess, on March 29, the defendants stood in the dock and listened to the senior judge give a list of "findings of fact."

One such finding was that the ANC and its allies had been working to replace the government with a "radically and fundamentally different form of state."

Another was that the ANC's program of action "envisaged the use of illegal means" and that illegal means had been used during the Defiance Campaign.

A third finding was that certain leaders of the ANC had made occasional speeches inciting violence, though the prosecution had failed to prove a policy of violence.

The last finding was that there was a strong left-wing tendency in the ANC, one that was "anti-imperialist, anti-West and pro-Soviet," but the prosecution had not proved that the ANC was Communist. Nine years after those charges had first been made, three and a half years after their trial had begun, the thirty-one defendants standing in the dock heard the judge say, "You are found not guilty and discharged. You may go."

Amid the cheers of their supporters, the defendants danced out of the courtroom, carrying their attorneys on their shoulders. Winnie was relieved about the verdict, but she was also worried. She knew that Nelson was not going to return home to stay. Scarcely a word had been spoken, but she knew in her heart that it would be a long, long time before he would be home to stay; if indeed he ever came home to stay again.

· 7 ·

Nelson Mandela
Goes Underground

During the time when they were imprisoned under the state of emergency, Nelson Mandela, Walter Sisulu, and the other defendants in the Treason Trial had taken advantage of the opportunity to be together without constant interruptions to formulate new plans for the African National Congress. Now that the organization was outlawed, they would have to use new tactics to get their message out to the people.

They made these new plans on the assumption that they would be found not guilty before too many more months went by. But even though they would be technically free, they knew they would be watched closely. As leaders of an outlawed organization, they could be arrested on the slightest suspicion of continuing the work of the ANC. This meant that they would have to keep a very low profile. But if they kept too quiet, the people would forget that the ANC existed. Therefore, at least one of them would have to continue the work of the ANC in defiance of the law. He would have to go underground, surfacing only for specific public actions. Nelson Mandela was chosen to be this outlaw.

He was the obvious choice, for he had long been one of the major heroes of the struggle and one of the most charismatic. He was also a man whose commitment to the struggle was so deep that he was willing to do whatever was necessary to further the cause. He apparently accepted the role he was to play without visibly showing any misgivings, but it was probably the most difficult decision he ever made in his life. He faced a time—he did not know how long—of being hunted continuously by the police, risking arrest and imprisonment or even death if he were caught. He would have to go for long stretches without seeing Winnie and the children, and there might be weeks when he would not even know if they were all right. This is what bothered him most, and in fact he could not bring himself to tell Winnie what he was about to do.

By mid-March, when the judge in the Treason Trial cut short the prosecutor's presentation and declared a week's recess, Nelson's plans were set. In fact, he was already doing as much as he could to provide for Winnie and the girls in his absence; but he had not said a thing to Winnie. She later recalled, "I think he found it too hard to tell me. With all that power and strength he exudes, he is so soft inside. I had just noticed that week that he was silent and thoughtful, and I remember asking whether anything was worrying him. And then, before washing his shirt one day, I found a document in the pocket. He had paid rent for six months—that was very unusual. So I think he was trying to ease the pain, trying to think of ways in which I would be able to face life more easily without him. And then the car. It was not in order, and he suddenly had it repaired, and just left it parked in the garage."

On the day the judge in the Treason Trial declared the one-week recess, Nelson came home accompanied by several of his co-defendants and friends, but he did not get beyond the gate. Nor could Winnie reach him through the crowd of people who surrounded him with cheers and congratulations. He called out to her to pack a few things for him in a suitcase, saying only that he would be "going away for a long time." Winnie did as he had asked, but by the time she took the suitcase outside he was gone. A friend came by for it about an hour later. Winnie had no idea where Nelson was.

The following day she read that he had given a speech at a convention in Pietermaritzburg and at first wondered how he had got permission to go outside the geographical limits imposed by his banning orders. Then it dawned on her that the ten-year banning orders that had been imposed in early March 1952 had expired. Nelson was actually free to travel anywhere he wanted to in South Africa. Apparently no one in the government had realized that either; otherwise they would most certainly have sought to renew the ban.

The meeting that convened at Pietermaritzburg on March 25, 1961, was called the All-In African Conference and was attended by some 1,400 delegates from all over South Africa. It had been called because at the end of May the new white Republic of South Africa would formally come into being; unlike the Union of South Africa that had been formed in 1910, it would have no formal association with Britain. Afrikaner Nationalists were in power now, and black South Africans were under no illusions about what that would mean for them. They issued a call for a National Convention of elected representatives "of all adult men and women on an equal basis irrespective of colour, creed or other limitation" to draw up a "new, non-racial democratic constitution for South Africa."

Addressing the delegates, who greeted him as a kind of savior, Nelson said, "We must win in the end," and later the delegates chose him to head a National Action Council to present their demands to the government. If the government refused to call such a convention, the delegates were prepared to urge demonstrations across the country, including a three-day stay-at-home to coincide with the official birth of the new Republic.

After Nelson left Pietermaritzburg, he met with Albert Lutuli to report on the convention. Then he returned to Pretoria on March 29 to hear the not-guilty verdict. There was no time to share the good news with his wife. From the court, he went underground.

Even in a virtual police state like South Africa, with a huge standing army, border checkpoints, and rigid pass-laws, there were many places where a black man could hide and many ways he could travel about. The ANC had been planning for Nelson's descent into the underground for several weeks, and a network of hiding places and helpers had been arranged. Naturally, the nature of this network and the identity of the helpers cannot be revealed, and even Winnie did not know the identity of the people, but, she says, they were mostly whites. With the aid of this network, he traveled throughout the country, and though the government had issued a warrant for his arrest, he moved about with considerable freedom.

He did not visit only black areas, but Indian and Muslim and Coloured areas as well, for he and the ANC understood that though many differences might divide these various groups, they had one major thing in common: they were not equal to whites under South African law and would not enjoy equality unless they acted together. Nelson's major concern in his first weeks as an outlaw was to attract support for the three-day "stay-at-home" which was to begin on the 29th of May. While this demonstration was supposed to take place only if the government failed to call the National Convention proposed at the Pietermaritzburg Conference, Nelson knew that the government would refuse. He wrote to both Prime Minister Verwoerd and to the leader of the United Party, made up mostly of English speakers and the opposition party to the controlling Nationalists in Parliament, but neither man replied. Not really expecting replies, Nelson continued his underground campaign.

He visited rural areas and urban areas, the Cape and Natal. He stayed in white homes and Indian homes as well as black homes. He went out almost exclusively at night, and in the mornings put on a sweat suit and jogged in place, since he could not run two miles as he would have liked. He disguised himself as a chauffeur and a window cleaner and a messenger, and he had several narrow escapes.

The narrowest came in November when, dressed in a chauffeur's uniform, he was waiting on a Johannesburg streetcorner for a car that was supposed to pick him up. A black security policeman approached him, and Nelson knew from the man's eyes that he had been recognized. To Nelson's astonishment, the man passed, giving him a wink and the thumbs-up salute of the ANC. The black security police in South Africa were notorious for their brutality against their own people. Nelson was lucky to have been recognized by the one black policeman among hundreds who would not give him away.

Given the conditions under which he had to live, he managed to see Winnie remarkably often, sometimes even in their own house, though always late at night because the police were watching closely. Winnie lived for what she called "that sacred knock" and learned to be prepared to go anywhere at any time she was summoned. Once, when she was having trouble with her car, she received a message to drive to a particular corner in Soweto. She did so, and a man in a chauffeur's uniform got in beside her. For a moment she did not recognize her husband. He drove her to a garage and bought her a new car, trading in the old one. Then he drove her to the center of Johannesburg, stopped at a red light, got out of the car, and disappeared into the crowd.

On many occasions, they met in cars on lonely roads at night, hoping that they would not get caught in one of the numerous roadblocks that the police set up whenever they heard that Nelson might be in a particular area. On one occasion they ran right into a roadblock, and the only thing that saved them was that Winnie was overweight. The lithe young girl who had been so athletic was now a woman who had borne two children and who had a job that involved a lot of sitting—at desks, in cars, in people's homes. Winnie describes herself as so heavy that she looked pregnant all the time, and when they were stopped at the roadblock she decided to take advantage of her appearance. She pretended that she was in labor and about to give birth at any moment. The police let the car pass.

As May 31, Republic Day, neared, pamphlets calling for

"the People of South Africa" to "stay at home" were distributed across the country. Reports from all over had Nelson Mandela showing up to speak at secret meetings, then disappearing before the police could capture him. Some of the newspapers played up the story of the romantic renegade urging his people to freedom. In response, the government staged a huge crackdown on all individuals and groups suspected of planning to participate in the three-day demonstration. There were 10,000 arrests, mostly of ordinary Africans, under the pass laws. Meetings were banned all across the country, and printing establishments suspected of printing Mandela's leaflets were raided. The white newspaper the *Rand Daily Mail* published what it said was a secret plan for nonwhites to invade the cities. Nelson and other ANC leaders believed that the government had deliberately planted that story to frighten whites. The newspapers failed to report Nelson's statement that no such plan ever existed.

On May 29, 1961, hundreds of thousands of blacks did stay at home, and in some areas they were joined by other racial minorities—by Indians in Durban and by Coloureds in Cape Town (the first time that Coloureds had ever actively participated in a black-organized demonstration). In some cities, including Johannesburg and Port Elizabeth, 60% to 75% of nonwhite people stayed at home. In other areas, the rate of absenteeism was not so good. It was hard for Nelson to judge, because he had to rely on his own sources, realizing that the newspapers were not likely to report the truth. He stated publicly that he thought the response "magnificent," considering the government's campaign to suppress the demonstration and the fact that the outlawed ANC had been forced to do all its organizing in secret; but on the second day he called a halt to the three-day strike.

What were he and the ANC going to do now? Nelson could not speak for the ANC, only for himself. He would continue to operate from the underground. "I will not leave South Africa, nor will I surrender."

In October, after countless meetings throughout the summer and early fall, Nelson and the other leaders of the ANC made a decision that they had hoped to avoid: they decided to try violence. There was no question in their minds that nonviolent measures could not work against a government like that of South Africa. Perhaps violence was the answer.

They did not turn the ANC into an organization committed to violence. They decided that the ANC as a whole would remain true to its original nonviolent principles, though from that time on it would no longer disapprove of violent acts so long as these acts were "properly controlled." A small group led by Nelson Mandela and including some Communist members of the ANC formed a new secret organization to be called Umkhonto we Sizwe (Spear of the Nation). They did not consult with Albert Lutuli or Walter Sisulu or many of the other ANC leaders because they did not want to compromise the nonviolent stance of the ANC.

Now that he was publicly committed to violence, no matter how "controlled," Nelson Mandela was in even greater danger than he had been before. Not only was he in danger of being turned in to the police by blacks or other nonwhites who still denounced violence; the police now would have no fear of killing him on the spot. Thus, it is ironic that at this time he had the opportunity to see Winnie and his daughters more than during the underground time when he had still been committed to nonviolence.

One day in November, Winnie received a message telling her to get the girls ready for a trip. They were soon picked up by a car, driven for a while, then transferred to another car, and then to another. Their final destination proved to be a farm in Rivonia on the outskirts of Johannesburg that had been rented for Umkhonto we Sizwe. Called Lilliesleaf, it had a number of outbuildings in addition to the main house, and in one of these outbuildings the family was reunited. For a few hours at a time they enjoyed life as a family. Winnie cooked meals; the children walked with their father in the garden. Young Zeni was not yet 3 years old, but she referred to the farm as "home" after that, for it was the only place where she had played with her father.

Meanwhile, the small band of members that made up Umkhonto we Sizwe discussed strategy and determined that attacks on buildings that would not endanger human life were the best actions to take. On December 16, 1961, bombs exploded in twenty-three symbolic economic targets—stores and other commercial buildings in Johannesburg, Port Elizabeth, and Durban. At the same time, leaflets were distributed announcing the existence of Umkhonto we Sizwe (MK) and its purpose:

> *We of Umkhonto have always sought—as the liberation movement has sought—to achieve liberation without bloodshed and civil clash. We hope, even at this late hour, that our first actions will awaken everyone to a realization of the disastrous situation to which the Nationalist policy is leading. We hope*

*that we will bring the government and its supporters
to their senses before it is too late, so that both the
government and its policies can be changed before
matters reach the desperate stage of civil war. . . .
The time comes in the life of any nation when there
remain only two choices: submit or fight. That time
has now come to South Africa. We shall not submit
and we have no choice but to hit back by all means
within our power in defence of our people, our future and our freedom.*

*The government has interpreted the peacefulness of
the movement as weakness; the people's non-violent
policies have been taken as a green light for government violence. . . . We are striking out along a new
road for the liberation of the people of this country.*

That same month the committee in Oslo, Norway, that
awards the Nobel prizes each year announced that Albert
Lutuli had been named the winner of the Nobel Prize for
Peace for leading the ANC in the nonviolent struggle
against apartheid. Lutuli accepted the prize on behalf of
the outlawed ANC less than a week before the MK bomb-
ings, and the coincidence of the two events was ironic.

In January 1962, Nelson Mandela left the land of his
birth for the first time. His old friend and law partner,
Oliver Tambo, the leader of the ANC in exile, had arranged for him to address a Pan-African Freedom Conference in Ethiopia. The night before he slipped out of the
country, Nelson managed to see Winnie. She could tell he
was excited. Never before in his life had he been out from
under the yoke of South Africa's laws. Outside the country, he would be able to move about freely without fear of

being arrested. Nelson had promised not to leave South Africa, but secretly Winnie wondered if he would return.

In Addis Ababa, Ethiopia, he gave the delegates at the conference a full report on conditions in South Africa and the struggle against apartheid. He urged his audience to do whatever was possible to put pressure on the South African government to change its policies, and applauded the limited sanctions that were already in place. These sanctions, or efforts to show disapproval of the Nationalist government's policies, were at the time mostly verbal expressions of disagreement. Nelson Mandela urged the nations represented at the conference to limit trade with South Africa and to break diplomatic relations with the country. He also explained why he had come to believe that violence was the most effective strategy against the government.

Back in South Africa, the authorities were furious to learn that Nelson Mandela had managed to slip across the border and was now attracting publicity and support outside the country. They could not do much about him, but they could take out their anger on those he had left behind.

Not long after her husband left the country, Winnie made a speech before the Indian Youth Congress. That was enough for the authorities. On January 28, Winnie was made a banned person. Under the banning orders imposed on her, she could not travel outside the Johannesburg district without permission, could not attend meetings, could not address gatherings of people, could not make statements to the press, and had to live under a variety of other restrictions. If she disobeyed any of them, she was subject to arrest and imprisonment.

After Addis Ababa, Nelson and Oliver Tambo went on a

tour of a number of states in North and West Africa. It was an exhilarating experience for Nelson, and for the first time he felt like a free man: "Free from white oppression, from the idiocy of apartheid and racial arrogance, from police molestation, from humiliation and indignity. Wherever I went I was treated like a human being. In the African states I saw black and white mingling peacefully and happily in hotels, cinemas; trading in the same areas, using the same public transport, and living in the same residential areas." He dreamed of the day when such a thing could happen in the land of his birth and wished that Winnie could have shared the experience with him. He did manage to write (friends smuggled the letters to her), and she was grateful that he had taken the time to do so.

He traveled to London where he met with the members of the ANC in exile who were based there. Then he returned to Africa where he visited Algeria in the north and then Tanzania, Zambia, and Kenya in East Africa. Since the ANC had been outlawed, groups of ANC supporters had slipped out of South Africa and set up bases in neighboring countries where young recruits were trained in military tactics and taught academic subjects that they had been denied the opportunity to learn under the Bantu Education laws. Plans were in the works to start farms so that these ANC bases would be self-supporting and also to give the recruits experience in running farms so that when they were able to return to South Africa as full-fledged citizens they would have the skills they needed to participate in the agricultural sector of the economy.

When Nelson slipped back over the border into South Africa, he was optimistic about what he had seen and renewed in his sense that the struggle would one day be successful. But it was hard for him to return to a country whose authorities wanted more than anything else to capture him. He realized that word would get out that he was back, and the campaign against him would grow even worse.

In Nelson's absence Umkhonto we Sizwe had engaged in more acts of sabotage, and the police had cracked down even more on suspected allies of the MK and ANC. Under the circumstances, Nelson decided that the best place to hide was right under the noses of the police, and the Johannesburg house in which he stayed for the first few days after his return was directly across the street from a police station.

Despite the danger, he managed also to see Winnie soon after his return. He had been away for eight months, the longest separation in a relationship that had seen them apart more than they were together. For Winnie, just touching her husband was a joy, and for the brief time she had with him she willed herself not to think about the danger they were in. He had managed to remain free for seventeen months, but both knew that the odds were against his remaining free much longer.

From Johannesburg, Nelson went to Durban to meet with the members of Umkhonto we Sizwe there. He traveled disguised as a chauffeur and driving a car that belonged to Cecil Williams, the white director of a theater in Johannesburg. Williams rode in the car as the "boss." On Sunday, August 5, 1962, they set off from Durban to drive to Johannesburg. On the way they were stopped by three carloads of police who, Williams later said, did not seem to know exactly whom they were looking for and who were astonished when they recognized the chauffeur as

Nelson Mandela. Williams, and others, believed that the police had been tipped off that someone very important was in that car.

The next day, Winnie was on her way out of the Child Welfare Society office when she saw one of the men who had driven her to some of her secret meetings with Nelson. The man was wild-eyed and agitated, and she knew immediately that something had happened to her husband. The only question she asked was, had he been injured? No, the man answered, he had not been injured. But he had been captured and would probably be formally charged in court the following day.

Winnie drove straight home, although later she could not remember anything about the short trip. She only knew she had to get home so she could think about what had happened, about what it meant. For the past seventeen months she had known her husband was in danger, but as long as he had remained free there had always been the possibility of seeing him, of touching him. Now that he had been captured, she knew that he would never be allowed to return home again. They might not execute him, but they would put him in prison. She would not be able to feel his arms around her. Her children would not be able to walk in a garden with him or play with him. She thought back over the few brief years they had known each other, over the many separations and the constant interruptions even when they had been together. As she later put it, "I had so little time to love him."

·8·

The Trial of Nelson Mandela

*N*elson Mandela was imprisoned at the Johannesburg Fort while he awaited being formally charged. Three days after his arrest, on August 8, 1962, he was taken to Magistrates' Court where he was charged with inciting African workers to strike and leaving the country without valid travel documents. These were the only charges the government had supporting evidence for—they suspected that he was connected with Umkhonto but could not prove it.

Nelson entered the courtroom slowly and with a big smile on his face. From her seat in the public gallery, Winnie felt as if her soul were reaching out to him. She watched and listened as the brief hearing established the formal charges and her husband stood proudly and silently and then, in handcuffs, was led away. Both prayed that he would never have to go to trial to face these charges. Nelson's friends were working on an escape plan that would take advantage of the daily movements between the Fort and the courtroom. Then the government announced that Nelson would not be tried in Johannesburg but in Pretoria, and the hope of his escaping was dashed, for his friends did not have the same underground network in operation in Pretoria as they had in Johannesburg.

The trial date was set for October 22. In the weeks before the trial, an international movement to free Mandela arose. People painted the slogan "Free Mandela!" on walls and fences. The foreign press printed articles describing him as a proud resistance fighter. Many South Africans, black and white, organized meetings to decide how best to pressure the government to free him. In response, the government banned any gathering that supported him.

When the trial opened, crowds gathered outside the Pretoria courtroom hoping to get a glimpse of him. In the courtroom itself, there was a buzz of anticipation. Winnie, who had received permission to attend the trial, could feel the electricity in the room. When Mandela entered the room there were cheers from the public gallery. Nelson wore a jackal-skin robe that had been presented to him by his supporters. He wore it like the royal chief he was. He grinned and raised his fist and called out "Amandla!" (Power!). His supporters responded with "Ngawethu!" (To the People!).

It was a very short trial. Mandela conducted his own defense and spent little time defending himself. Rather, he used the occasion to make political statements. As he told the magistrate, "I hope to be able to indicate that this case is a trial of the aspirations of the African people, and because of that I thought it proper to conduct my own defense." He also said, "I consider myself neither legally nor morally bound to obey laws made by a parliament in which I have no representation." He pleaded not guilty to both charges, but he, and everyone else, had little doubt about the outcome of the trial. On October 25, just three days after its beginning, Nelson was found guilty on both charges.

Nelson had the opportunity to address the court before sentence was passed. He gave a long address that traced his involvement in the struggle, his years of being banned even though he had not been either tried or convicted, and the hardships of life as an outlaw. Toward the end he said, "It has not been easy for me during the past period to separate myself from my wife and children . . . and instead to take up the life of a man hunted continuously by the police, living separated from those who are closest to me, in my own country, facing continually the hazards of detection and of arrest. This has been a life infinitely more difficult than serving a prison sentence. No man in his right senses would voluntarily choose such a life in preference to the one of normal, family, social life which exists in every civilized country. But there comes a time, as it came in my life, when a man is denied the right to live a normal life, when he can only live the life of an outlaw because the government had so decreed to use the law to impose a state of outlawry upon him. I was driven to this situation, and I do not regret having taken the decisions I did take."

When he finished, the spectators cheered, and Winnie felt so very proud of her husband, and so grateful that in the midst of his troubles he still thought of her and the children. She prayed that he would not be sentenced to a long prison term when the court reconvened to pass sentence on November 7.

Nelson Mandela was sentenced to five years in prison, three for inciting workers to strike and two for leaving the country without valid travel documents. His face betrayed no emotion. He said, "I have no doubt that posterity will pronounce me innocent, and that the criminals that should have been brought before this court are the members of the Verwoerd Government." As he left the court, he cried, "Amandla!" three times, and three times his supporters roared back, "Ngawethu!"

As Winnie left the courthouse, reporters swarmed around her and cameras clicked in her face. She forced herself to smile and to say with determination, "I will continue the fight as I have in all ways done in the past."

Nelson was taken back to Fort Johannesburg briefly, then transferred to Pretoria Central Prison. Before leaving for Pretoria, he had a chance to smuggle out a letter to Winnie. In it, he told her how much he loved her and the children and asked her to be strong. They faced years of separation, and she faced years of being without his protection. He warned her to beware of traps, of people who appeared to be friends but who were really enemies, of gossip and slander designed to cause her to lose faith. He reminded her that they had both expected his arrest and imprisonment at some point. He urged her to continue the struggle in his absence.

It was a wonderful letter, and Winnie read it over and over. She would like to have kept it always, finding comfort in its words, but it was later seized by the police in one of the frequent raids on her home, and to this day she has never been able to get it back.

Not long after Nelson was sentenced, Winnie realized that the authorities would love an excuse to charge him with more serious crimes. For one thing, they began to raid her home. Usually, it was in the middle of the night. There was a banging at the door, and when she opened it she was pushed aside by security police who ransacked her belongings, seized her papers, and frightened Zeni and Zindzi. Sometimes, the police would take her away for questioning and try to break her will, hoping somehow to trick her into betraying her husband.

She was prepared for this. She was not as prepared for some of the other traps the authorities would lay, but in his letter Nelson had warned her to be wary, and she tried to remember his warning. Even before Nelson was moved to Pretoria, she was offered the opportunity to finance his escape. A man whom she and Nelson considered a friend assured her that he could arrange such an escape for a price. Winnie listened to the plan, which called for Nelson to cut through the bars of his prison cell with a saw provided by a prison officer and then make his escape with a gun provided by the same officer.

As she listened, Winnie wondered how in the world such a plan could work. Wouldn't he make an awful lot of noise sawing through iron bars? How would Nelson, with a single revolver, manage to get past a host of armed prison officers? But she said only that she would have to see about raising the money. Then she went immediately to Walter Sisulu to tell him about the offer. Sisulu was sure the plan was really a trap for her and Nelson. It would give the authorities an excuse to kill him and arrest her. He told her not to return to the Fort, and she did not.

While she worried constantly that other plots against herself and her husband were being hatched by the authorities, Winnie at least tried to comfort herself with the idea that if Nelson survived his five-year sentence, the family might be reunited again. In the meantime, it was up to her to support her family. She continued in her job at the Child Welfare Society and tried to make a normal home life for her daughters, who were too young to understand what had happened. Zeni, three years old, did know that her father had been taken by the police, but she didn't really know what that meant. She would soon feel the effect of being Nelson Mandela's daughter, however.

Winnie decided to put Zeni in nursery school and enrolled her in a private Catholic school in nearby Kliptown. Four weeks later, Winnie received a letter advising her that the child of Nelson Mandela could not remain at the school. Little Zeni had enjoyed going to the school, and it was difficult for Winnie to tell her that she could not return there. Winnie then placed the child in a private Indian school.

Meanwhile, racial unrest in South Africa continued, spurred in part by international opinion against apartheid. On November 6, 1962, the day before Nelson was sentenced, the General Assembly of the United Nations had voted to impose sanctions against South Africa. Real action could come only after a similar vote in the UN Security Council, which was not likely to happen anytime soon, since Britain and the United States held votes in the Security Council and they were opposed to official sanctions. Still, the General Assembly vote was important as a symbol of world opinion.

In South Africa, Umkhonto continued its work, especially in the Eastern Cape where it was strongest. Acts of sabotage were committed not only against whites but against those blacks who were cooperating in the government's drive to establish Bantu homelands. In response, the government imposed even more drastic measures to stifle dissent, allowing security police to detain people without trial and in solitary confinement for up to ninety days, and allowing the police to harass anyone suspected of ties to Umkhonto or the ANC. Walter Sisulu was arrested several times and sentenced to prison for furthering the aims of the ANC. While out on bail pending appeal, he went underground in April 1963.

Nelson Mandela was transferred from Pretoria Central Prison to Robben Island, a penal settlement off Cape Town, and placed in solitary confinement. The authorities gave as their reason the racial unrest and their suspicion that Mandela was somehow still involved in Umkhonto. In June, Winnie was given permission to visit him there.

She traveled over 700 miles from Johannesburg to Cape Town, then another six miles on the ferry from Cape Town to Robben Island. She was escorted into a shack that had been built at the shore. Nelson was then brought to the shack. A double-wire mesh separated them, and they were forced to stand during the thirty minutes they were allowed together. They were forbidden to speak in Xhosa, in case they wanted to say anything that the white authorities who stood alongside them would not understand, so they spoke in English. They could not touch. But both were pleased and relieved to see one another, to know with their own eyes that the other was well. At least Nelson was as well as could be expected, given that the food was bad and he was allowed no privileges. When she returned to Johannesburg, Winnie began a long fight for better conditions for her husband.

She also returned to find that their home had been ransacked again.

The month following Winnie's visit to Robben Island, the ANC and Umkhonto received a severe blow. Acting on the tip of an informant, the security police raided Lilliesleaf, the farm in Rivonia, outside Johannesburg, that served as Umkhonto's headquarters, and where Nelson had arranged visits with his family during his months underground. There they found and arrested Walter Sisulu and eight others; several more men were picked up later. The group, accused of sabotage and being organizers of Umkhonto, included whites and Indians as well as blacks. Later, two whites and two Indians managed to escape from Marshall Square Police Station in Johannesburg. Winnie, who was following the situation closely, was pleased to learn of the escape. But then she learned that another defendant had been added to the list of people charged in what became known as the Rivonia case— her husband, Nelson Mandela.

According to the security police, documents found at Lilliesleaf implicated Mandela in Umkhonto. He was moved from Robben Island to Pretoria Central Prison to be formally charged with the others accused. Altogether, they numbered eight—one white, one Indian, and six Africans, including Sisulu and Mandela. Mandela was Accused No. 1.

Formal charges were presented on October 1, 1963.

Winnie was not present at the Palace of Justice in Pretoria; she had applied for permission to travel there, but her application had been denied. Since July, all the defendants had been kept in solitary confinement, and they looked drawn and haggard to the hundreds of spectators who crowded into the courtroom, determined to witness the event in spite of police attempts at intimidating them by taking down their names and photographing them.

Defense attorney Bram Fischer led the hearing with an attack on the government's indictment, saying it contained absurd charges, including charges that Nelson Mandela had been involved in acts of sabotage while he was in prison. The judge agreed and threw out the indictment. Legally, the defendants were free. But then a security police lieutenant stepped into the prisoners' dock, thumped each man on the back, and declared, "I am arresting you on a charge of sabotage!" Prisoners again, they were taken back to their cells.

On December 3, 1963, the men were brought again to the Palace of Justice. This time the government presented "amended charges": recruiting persons for training in sabotage and guerrilla warfare for the purpose of violent revolution; conspiring to aid foreign military units when they invaded the Republic, thus furthering the aims of Communism; soliciting and receiving funds for these purposes from Algeria, Ethiopia, Liberia, Nigeria, Tunisia, and elsewhere.

Each defendant approached the dock to give his plea. As Accused No. 1, Nelson Mandela went first. "The government should be in the dock, not me," he said. "I plead not guilty." The others did the same. This time, Winnie had been granted permission to travel to Pretoria. When Nelson smiled at her, she felt revitalized.

Winnie had taken great care with her dress for the occasion. She was clothed in a full-length beaded dress of the Royal Thembu line. She made such a striking impression that the Minister of Justice immediately served her with a notice banning her from the courtroom if she appeared again in traditional dress. She obeyed the order, but always wore the black, green, and gold colors of the African National Congress. Meanwhile, Nelson's female relatives, including his mother and aunts, as well as other black women who attended the trial, showed their opinion of the order against Winnie by always wearing traditional costumes to the court.

It took every ounce of spirit she had for Winnie to go through that trial. It was a long one, and she had responsibilities at home as well as to her husband. She would get up before dawn, get the girls ready, drop them off at the home of a friend, then go to her office at the Child Welfare Society to put in a few hours' work before speeding off to Pretoria to attend as much as she could of the trial before speeding back to Johannesburg to pick up her children and be back at home by six o'clock so as to obey her banning orders. She did this for eleven months.

Meanwhile, her husband and the other defendants had decided unanimously not to try to defend themselves against the specific charges against them but to make the trial a political forum for attacking the apartheid system. Nelson Mandela became their natural leader and was the major spokesman for the group. When the defense finally began to present its case, on April 23, 1964, he spoke eloquently of the struggle, saying at the outset, "I want to say that the suggestion made by the State that the struggle in South Africa is under the influence of foreigners and Communists is wholly incorrect. I have done whatever I did, both as an individual and as a leader of my people, because of my experience in South Africa and my own proudly felt African background, and not because of what any outsider might have to say."

He spoke at great length, a total of about four hours. During the entire time, he held his audience spellbound. He boldly set forth what Africans wanted—equal political rights. He also stated that this would not lead to black domination, as whites feared. "The ANC has spent half a century fighting against racialism," he said. "When it triumphs, it will not change that policy."

He concluded very quietly, looking directly at the judge: "During my lifetime I have dedicated myself to this struggle of the African people. I have fought against white domination, and I have fought against black domination. I have cherished the ideal of a democratic and free society in which all persons live together in harmony and with equal opportunities. It is an ideal which I hope to live for and to achieve. But if needs be, it is an ideal for which I am prepared to die."

This was no idle statement on Mandela's part. The charges against him and the other defendants were so serious that, if found guilty, they could well be sentenced to death. All they could do was wait for the judge's decision. It was announced in early June.

Two days before the verdict was announced, Winnie was approached by some elders from Nelson's village who were intent on using a traditional method to save him.

They offered her a tiny bottle containing a brownish, oily liquid with what looked like a few hairs in it. She was to put it in her shoe and enter the courtroom, and it would protect her husband. Winnie looked at the elders, whom she had always been taught to respect, and at the bottle, and could not bring herself to take it. She knew that herbs and hairs were not going to free her husband, and besides, he was a fighter and certainly did not want any help from herbs. She refused the bottle and entered the courtroom. There, the judge handed down his decisions—the one white defendant was acquitted, the others were found guilty. Sentencing was set for June 12.

The elders blamed Winnie. She later recalled their reactions: "There you are! You see! A young thing like this did not want him released from jail!" They were convinced that she had "sold him to the white man." Later, looking back, she realized that she could have saved herself, and the elders, much heartache by simply taking the little bottle as they asked. But she had been too immature to understand that taking the bottle would have done far more good than harm.

The days between Nelson's conviction and sentencing were tense ones for Winnie. She worried about how much she had offended the elders. She worried over what sentence Nelson would receive. She made plans to take five-year-old Zeni and four-year-old Zindzi with her to Pretoria to hear the sentencing, for she was unsure when, if ever, they would see their father again. She tried to occupy her mind with these arrangements, and not to think about what fate might be in store for her husband, and for herself and the girls.

She was fairly sure that the defendants would not be

given the death sentence. There was great international pressure; in fact, the United Nations General Assembly had passed a resolution urging South African authorities to free the Rivonia defendants. There was also great unrest in South Africa, and she felt that the government must realize that it would invite revolution if the death sentence were passed. But hearing the sentence of life imprisonment was no cause for rejoicing. Some of the most important leaders in the struggle would no longer be able to lead. Without them it would be very difficult to regroup and reorganize the resistance.

But Winnie showed no despair as she left the courtroom. Instead, she held her head high and flashed a dazzling smile. The crowds of Africans who jammed the square cheered her, and she was moved by their affection. She realized that now she was indeed a symbol of her husband, and she must be a proud symbol to the people.

Winnie had no chance to be with Nelson after the sentence was passed. With hundreds of others, she and her daughters stood outside the courthouse, waiting to wave goodbye to him for the last time. The crowd swelled around them. They were singing freedom songs, and for a few moments Winnie felt buoyed by the sheer spirit of their numbers and of their determination to be free someday. But then a large security policeman grabbed her and reminded her that she was due back in Johannesburg in accordance with her banning orders. Winnie kicked him. She could not believe he had the gall to think of permits and the time of day when her husband had just been sentenced to life imprisonment.

She saw Nelson once before he was returned to Robben Island to begin his life sentence. "It was extremely painful," she later recalled. "But he has this way about him of reassuring you and dispelling whatever fears you have. Just seeing him reconstructed those emotions that were falling apart and rebuilt me. He prepared me for the difficult life ahead. In fact, almost everything that has happened in the last twenty years, he prophesied. He told me, you will be vilified, you must expect that you will be told you are responsible for my being in prison. You are young and life without a husband is full of all kinds of insults. I expect you to live up to my expectations."

Twenty-seven-year-old Winnie, mother of two small children, promised that she would. But she knew as she listened to her husband's words that she would never again be complete, that something profound would be lost when he was escorted from her. As she later described it, "Part of my soul went with him."

·9·

Life Without
Nelson Mandela

"Solitude, loneliness, is worse than fear—the most* wretchedly painful illness the body and mind could be subjected to," Winnie said later, referring to the first few weeks and months after Nelson was taken away. It was a terrible time for her. Not only did she worry about him, for she knew that he was experiencing a profound solitude and loneliness, too; but she also worried about herself. She felt that she was completely dependent upon him, even if he had not been around very much during their all-too-brief time together. She regarded herself as a shadow of him. During the first six months of his imprisonment he was allowed to write only one letter to her. Winnie, who had learned the hard way to be very careful with his letters, found a special hiding place for it and read it over and over again.

She was deeply depressed. In public, and for her daughters, she appeared strong. But inside, in private, she despaired. The government seemed determined to break her down. Everyone who tried to help her was subjected to police harassment and slander in the pro-government press. Worse still, when these people were men, there were always rumors that she was having affairs with them. A photographer named Peter Magubane did a great deal to help Winnie and her daughters, and as a result he was often detained and questioned. Newspapers ran stories with headlines like, FINDING A MAN IN MANDELA'S HOUSE, and Winnie knew that someone would see to it that Nelson got a copy of that particular paper in prison. Nelson had warned Winnie that such things would happen, and she determined that she would not allow them to break her spirit.

She was allowed to visit him at Robben Island after he had been there about two months. By this time so many political prisoners were there that the authorities had built a better place for visits. There was a glass partition now, and seats, and prisoners and visitors spoke to one another by two-way telephones. Winnie yearned to be able to touch Nelson, but she took comfort in looking into his eyes and hearing his deep and sonorous voice. As always, he urged her to be brave and strong, and she went away feeling that she could live up to his expectations. But on her return home she found that her home had been invaded and searched again.

Her family realized how she was feeling, and some of them tried to help. Her older sister Nancy was close by, and visited often. Nancy, too, was involuntarily separated from her husband, Sefton Vuthela. While working at the University of Witwatersrand he had been banned for his political activities. Charged with violating his banning order, he escaped to neighboring Botswana rather than be sent to prison. Later, Nancy and her two children would be smuggled across the border to join him. But for the time being Nancy provided much-needed companionship and strength to Winnie.

A younger brother, Msuthu, had recently graduated from high school, and he traveled from the Transkei to Johannesburg to stay with Winnie and try to help out. But pretty soon the police raided Winnie's home and discovered Msuthu there. He did not have a permit to be in Johannesburg, and he was arrested and charged with being in an urban area without valid documents.

The newspapers reported the arrest in big headlines, and Columbus Madikizela was furious. He called Winnie and accused her of using his son for political purposes. Now Winnie was furious. She told her father that he might have sold out to the whites, but that she never would, and that none of his children had an obligation to sell out as he had. It was the first time she had ever spoken to her father with such disrespect, and it had a strange effect on her. After that, some of her old spirit returned, her depression began to lift, she started to get on with her life.

Both Zeni and Zindzi were of school age now, and Winnie was determined that they not receive the poor Bantu education decreed by the government. Through a relative of Nelson's, Judith Mtirara, who was light-skinned, Winnie managed to enroll her daughters in a school that was supposed to be for Coloured, or mixed-race, children. This was against the law, and so she was unable to take them to the school herself or visit them there. She had to rely on Judith to do that. In fact, the girls were enrolled under the names Zeni and Zindzi Mtirara, which, in the extended family network to which Nelson belonged, was perfectly all right.

The girls liked the school and did well there. But after a while the security police became suspicious and followed them to the school. Once they found out the two black girls were attending a school for Coloured children, they threatened to close down the school for breaking the law. The girls had to leave.

By this time, young Zeni was beginning to wonder why she kept having to leave schools she liked, why she did not have a father at home as other children did. One day she asked her mother why, if her father was in prison because he was fighting for black people, the father next door was not also in prison? She wanted to know why they couldn't go to a school and stay there. Winnie answered these difficult questions as best she could, but she realized that as they grew older the girls would have even more questions, and problems. As the daughters of Nelson Mandela, they would not have a chance to grow up normally.

Winnie now decided that the girls should go to school outside the country, in spite of the hardships it would cause for them and for her. She hated the idea of being separated from them, but she realized that they were not living a normal life with her. More than once, they had watched the security police take her away in the middle of the night. Before long, they too would start being taken away for questioning, for the South African security police were notoriously brutal to black children. Through a friend, she arranged for them to attend a Catholic girls' school in neighboring Swaziland, the Convent of Our Lady of Sorrows. It was a place of harsh discipline, and the girls were miserable. Eventually, they transferred to Waterford, an exclusive private school in Swaziland, an independent kingdom on South Africa's northeast border. Sir Robert Birley and his wife, Lady Birley, helped with the arrangements and the fees.

Winnie met this British couple at the University of Witwatersrand. A group of students there had organized a program of correspondence courses for Nelson Mandela and other political prisoners at Robben Island. The authorities had ordered the students to stop, but then another group had taken over. Sir Robert Birley was then a visiting professor at the university, and he was among the group who took over from the students. Winnie became friends with him and his wife, and when she confided her misgivings about the convent school that her daughters attended, Lady Birley suggested that they enroll at Waterford and offered to help pay their fees. Other friends paid the fees at private schools outside the country for Nelson's sons from his first marriage, whom Winnie also worried about and tried to be a loving stepmother to, as much as she was able.

Winnie needed all the financial help she could get at this time, for she had lost her job at the Child Welfare Society. She was shocked to learn that the security police had been pressuring the officials at the society to fire her ever since she had been hired. In fact, while the government subsidized the salaries of the other workers at the society, they had refused to do so with hers, and for the four years she worked there her salary had been paid out of the Society's own funds. But now the government made it impossible to continue working at her job.

In June 1965, for no apparent reason, she was issued new and even more stringent banning orders. Now she could not travel, even in the daytime, outside of Orlando

Township, where she lived. Sadly, her boss at the Child Welfare Society told her that she would have to leave, but if her banning orders were relaxed they would take her back immediately.

Winnie had to work to pay for food. She got a job as a clerk in a furniture shop. Two months later she was fired, for the security police had put pressure on her boss. This happened over and over again, as the authorities sought to break her by denying her even the opportunity to work. She briefly held a job at a correspondence college for black journalists; she lost that one because her banning orders prevented her from "entering educational premises." She worked at a dry cleaners, at a shoe shop, for a lawyer. None of these jobs lasted long.

Journalist friends who wanted to help suggested that she might make money by writing articles. The authorities apparently found out about the idea and in 1966 issued new banning orders prohibiting Winnie from writing or publishing anything. They kept up a steady barrage of harassment, barging into her home and arresting her at all hours of the night on suspicion of violating one banning order or another. She was arrested twice in 1967, but given a suspended sentence.

That same year Chief Albert Lutuli was killed by a train as he crossed a railroad bridge. The authorities claimed that his deafness prevented him from hearing the train. His family, and others, suspected that he had been deliberately run over.

One way or another, nearly all the leaders of the ANC had been taken care of by the authorities. Nelson Mandela and the others at Robben Island worked at hard labor on the island's rock piles and hoped for the day when political events on the outside might bring about their release. The one remaining ANC leader who continued to be somewhat effective was Oliver Tambo, in exile. He became President-General of the ANC and did all he could to attract support and funds around the world. But there was only so much he could do from afar. The struggle was in a sorry state.

Nelson Mandela refused to give up hope, however. He realized that it was the one thing the authorities could not take away from him, and he nourished it in himself. He was determined to keep himself fit and exercised daily; he even came to regard his work lifting heavy rocks as exercise that was good for keeping in shape. Eventually, he secured permission to cultivate a small garden, and he wrote Winnie a couple of letters about his tomato plants. In one, he told of a tomato plant that he had carefully nurtured and then accidentally injured and caused to die. He wrote that he had felt very bad about that and had pulled up the injured plant and washed its roots and thought of the life that might have come from them.

His letters could be no longer than 500 words, and they could not contain anything political, so Winnie believed that he sometimes wrote about nonpolitical things, hoping she would understand that he was really writing about politics. She felt that when he wrote about that tomato plant he was really writing about the struggle, about how he had tried to bring it to maturity and about how badly he felt that it was in such disarray.

After a time, partly through the efforts of Winnie and others, Nelson and his fellow political prisoners at Robben Island were allowed to take correspondence courses.

Nelson took additional courses in law, knowing that he must continue to exercise his mind as well as his body. They were not allowed to read newspapers, but they managed to develop a network inside the prison that allowed them to keep up with events on the outside and occasionally to get messages out. One way they kept up on current news was talking to newly arrived political prisoners. They also learned that the prison authorities nearly always treated them more severely when something the authorities didn't like happened on the outside.

Liberation struggles in other black African former colonies seemed to bring out the worst in the prison guards. Every time the rebels in Angola, Mozambique, and Namibia engaged in armed struggles with the ruling parties, Nelson and his fellow prisoners were denied privileges, beaten, and otherwise made to pay for what was going on elsewhere.

In 1965, Bram Fischer, who had defended Nelson and the others in the Rivonia trial, was arrested and charged with being the leader of the illegal South African Communist Party. He went underground and managed to evade capture for nearly a year. But the government passed a law that allowed the security police to pick up anyone they wanted to and to detain him or her in solitary confinement for 180 days. Pretty soon they had the information they needed to find Fischer. He was convicted of conspiring with the Rivonia defendants and sentenced to life imprisonment. He was sent to Pretoria Central Prison, where white political prisoners were held.

In 1966 Prime Minister Hendrik Verwoerd was killed by a deranged white messenger in the National Assembly. He was succeeded by B. J. Vorster. Nelson did not expect the policies of the government to change to any great degree under Vorster's leadership.

But he could not give up hope. Nor could Winnie. They lived their separate lives—he in prison, she under strict banning orders—holding on to whatever hope they could muster as if their very lives depended on it. And in a very real way, they did.

·10·

In Pretoria Prison

*I*n early 1969 Oliver Tambo, the newly elected President-General of the ANC, traveled to Tanzania to meet with delegates to the Organization of African Unity. Founded in 1963 at Addis Ababa, Ethiopia, it consisted of thirty-two independent African nations and had as its stated purposes cooperation among those states and aiding the fight against colonial rule in those countries that were not yet independent. Also present at that meeting were delegates from the rebel groups in Tanzania, Mozambique, and Angola. All the delegates pledged full support for the ANC's struggle for freedom.

The South African government reacted quickly to this new threat, passing a new "Terrorism" Act. Under this new Act, anyone suspected of aiding terrorism (by which was meant anything against the government) could be arrested and detained in solitary confinement not for just 180 days but indefinitely. And the security police did not have to prove to anyone that they had a good basis for their suspicions.

Winnie immediately began to fear what this would mean for herself, and for Nelson. She fully expected to be detained. She also believed that the prison authorities would be rougher on him. All this worry caused her heart to beat too fast, and she went to a heart specialist to see what could be done. The doctor told her she had a heart condition and that she must try very hard not to become overexcited. Winnie wondered how in the world she was going to do that.

In the second week of May 1969, ten-year-old Zeni and nine-year-old Zindzi Mandela were home with Winnie during a school holiday. At 2:00 A.M. on May 12, all were asleep in their beds when the security police began to bang on the door and shine flashlights in the windows. They kicked in the door and ordered Winnie to get dressed and to accompany them for questioning. As her daughters cried and pleaded with the police to leave her alone, Winnie was hustled away.

Winnie was one of the first prisoners taken under the new Terrorism Act. The police took her to Pretoria Central Prison and shoved her into a cell with both an inside door and an outside door, separated by grilles. It was such an armored cell that she was certain that it was a death cell for prisoners who would be executed. She believed she was the only prisoner in that cell block. Later, she would learn that there were others—that twenty others had been arrested at the same time as she, and that they included a poet and a trade unionist, and that most had been involved in organizing aid for families of political prisoners. Over the next few weeks, hundreds of others would be detained. But she did not know that. She had no communication with other human beings, and she felt entirely alone.

Her cell contained a plastic bucket of water, a sanitary bucket, three blankets, and a straw mat. One of the first things she did was to draw a calendar on the wall so she could keep track of the date. Time passed very slowly in solitary confinement, and since the light in her cell was kept on during the night and off during the day, she had trouble knowing whether it was night or day. She could tell the time of day only by the meals that were served, like coffee and porridge in the morning. When meals were brought to her, it was a welcome break, though it was frightening to hear the jangling of keys in the several locks and to realize how hard it was even for the guards to reach her. The guards, who were women, would turn the lid of Winnie's sanitary bucket upside down and place the plate of food on it, and so Winnie, who had inherited a lot of her own mother's attitudes toward cleanliness, would not eat. No one told her what the charges were against her, how long she would be held, where her children were.

Winnie tried to hold on to her sanity. She understood that the authorities wanted to terrorize her, to crush her spirit so that when they questioned her she would be willing to give answers. But it was so lonely in that cell. She recalls that she welcomed even an ant or a fly as company. One day she found two ants, and she happily spent hours just watching them and playing with them, feeling that she was part of their world, at least.

Finally, two weeks later, a lieutenant named Swanepoel in the security police began to interrogate Winnie. When he grew tired, others took his place. But Winnie was allowed no rest. She was questioned continually for five days and nights, not allowed to sleep. While she was brought food, she could not eat, so she merely drank water for the entire five days. After a couple of days, she began to faint every few hours, worn down by lack of sleep and food. Each time, her interrogators would revive her and begin the questioning all over again. Eventually, she put aside her pride and pleaded for relief, showing her interrogators her swollen feet and hands. They laughed and told her that she had too much information to die on them.

They wanted to know about the ANC and its "Communist" contacts. They said they knew that her husband was sending her "instructions" from Robben Island and that she was responsible for inciting people to commit political acts against the government. They seemed to know about every secret meeting she had attended, every telephone call she had made or received. They told her that they had detained many of the people who had helped her and that they would keep them in prison indefinitely unless she confessed that she had influenced them. Finally, at the end of five days, Winnie gave in. She told Lieutenant Swanepoel that she would accept responsibility for everything if he would only release those others. Back in her cell, she slept for what seemed like days.

Later, Winnie stated that only then did she understand the absolute fear and hatred that the Afrikaners felt for blacks. As hardened as she thought she was, this kind of hate was something even she had never encountered. Later also, she learned that by comparison with other prisoners arrested under the Terrorism Act, and also held in Pretoria Central Prison, she had got off lightly. Others had been hung by their wrists and beaten, forced to stand until they dropped, tortured until they died. She realized that she had been spared this treatment partly because the security police believed she had more valuable information than the others but partly, too, because the police did not want to make her a martyr and provoke a black rebellion.

After interrogating her for five days, Lieutenant Swanepoel ordered Winnie back to her cell. She did not know if she would be charged and brought to trial. She did not know how much longer she would be kept in solitary confinement. It was terrible not knowing. All she could do was try to keep her sanity. She did start eating, although the food she was given was barely enough to keep starvation at bay. She later said, "We didn't get the same food as Coloured prisoners and the Indians. They get tea, coffee, bread and sugar. 'Bantu' get porridge without sugar, and something pitch black with lumps in it supposed to be coffee." She exercised daily on her mat. She pulled threads from her blankets and braided them. She tried to keep track of the days on the calendar she had scratched on the wall of her cell.

About two months after she had been arrested, Lieutenant Swanepoel came to her cell and asked her who Thembi Mandela was. When she answered that Thembi was her stepson, the lieutenant told her that Thembi had been killed in an automobile accident. Then he left. Winnie cried for the first time since her arrest. She cried because such a promising young man whom she had grown to love had been killed so young, but she cried especially because she realized how deeply the news would affect her husband. She yearned to be with him to comfort him; but she did not know if he even knew what had happened to her. She worried all over again about Zeni and Zindzi—had they heard? Did they know where she was? Were they all right?

Oddly, that tragedy brought to Winnie the first good news she'd had since being arrested: there were other prisoners in her cell block, and they sympathized with her and supported her.

One day as she lifted her plate of food from the top of her sanitary bucket, she noticed a piece of silver paper at the bottom of the bucket. It was stuck into the remains of her excrement (the bucket had not been thoroughly cleaned, but she was used to that). She took it out and opened it. There was writing on the white lining of the silver paper, a message from her fellow prisoners: "Mother of a Nation," it said, "we are with you." They were the first kind words she had received in two months.

Sitting in her bare, cold cell, Winnie did not feel like the Mother of a Nation. But she realized that other black people regarded her in that way. She was a heroine of the struggle, just as her husband was its hero. That brief message gave her renewed hope.

She did not have a pencil or pen, but she took a pin and pricked some words of thanks in the silver paper, and replaced it in the sanitary bucket.

From then on, she received occasional messages, once pricked with a pin on a banana skin. She cherished these contacts with other, caring human beings.

Five months after her arrest, Winnie was allowed to bathe properly and not to have to use her daily five-cup bucket of drinking water to wash with as well. She was also given a Bible. She realized that something had happened. Only later did she learn that her husband, who had been given no news of what had happened to her, had finally instructed his lawyers to go all the way to the South African Supreme Court if they had to, to find out. They did have to go that far, and the Supreme Court ordered that Winnie and the others in detention be given basic necessities.

Soon afterward, in October, Winnie and eighteen others who had been arrested at the same time as she were finally charged. While they had been detained under the Terrorism Act, they were charged under the Suppression of Communism Act. The charges against Winnie included: that she had been receiving instructions from her husband; and that she had revived the African National Congress by recruiting for the ANC, finding targets for sabotage, distributing banned literature, and using funerals to further the aims of the ANC; being in touch with guerrillas and encouraging hostility between whites and nonwhites.

Winnie was not present to hear the charges. Suffering from severe malnutrition, she was in the prison hospital, not in the court.

Lieutenant Swanepoel had forced Winnie and the others to agree to be represented in court by an attorney named Mendil Levin. But she, and they, knew that Nelson was working to have a well-known Johannesburg political lawyer named Joel Carlson represent them. On the day the trial opened, Carlson appeared to tell the judge that he had been hired by Winnie's husband to defend her but that he had not been permitted to see her. The judge gave Carlson permission to talk to the defendants, and they all stated that they did not want to be represented by Levin.

When the trial began, the State announced that it had

eighty witnesses against Winnie, including her youngest sister, Nonyaniso. But when the first twenty testified and were then questioned by Joel Carlson, all stated that they had been threatened and tortured into testifying against Winnie. After that the judge ordered a recess in the trial, and Winnie and the others were returned to solitary confinement.

Two months later, on February 16, 1970, they were brought back to court. The Attorney General told the court that the State was dropping the case against Winnie and the other defendants. The judge turned to the defendants and said, "I find you not guilty and you are discharged."

But before they could even realize what had happened, Winnie and the others were rearrested.

Once again they were not told why, except that they were being arrested, again, under the Terrorism Act. They were returned to solitary confinement, this time for seven months. Through Joel Carlson at the trial, and also through the prison grapevine, Winnie learned that her detention had caused international outrage. She did not see until much later The New York Times article of February 25, 1970, which stated, "The prosecution's strategy seems clear. It will simply hold the defendants under the Terrorism Act until more 'evidence' can be obtained or concocted by the bestial methods that have become a hallmark of South African 'justice.'"

Winnie spent seven more months in solitary confinement. During this time, she regained her spirit, and with other prisoners in her cell block engaged in a protest against the food they were being served. They banged on their cell doors and went on a hunger strike. They did not win any improvement in their food as a result, but they were at least doing something.

Meanwhile, relatives and friends on the outside, who had been shocked at the defendants' immediate rearrest after being acquitted of all charges, mounted a campaign for better treatment of the prisoners. Winnie and the others were allowed visits from relatives and friends, who brought food, and news from the outside. Attorneys for the prisoners took their complaints about prison conditions to court, and on rare occasions Winnie and the others had the opportunity to leave their cells to appear in court on these issues. Prison guards seemed to delight in humiliating them on these occasions. For one such court appearance, Winnie's relatives brought her a suitcase containing clothes and makeup. But before she could put on either, the guards dumped them on the floor of her cell and smeared the cosmetics all over the floor.

At last, in September, Winnie and the others came to trial again. Their attorneys pointed out to the judge that of the 540 charges in the new indictment against them, 526 were identical to those at the first trial except for a few changes in wording. If they had been acquitted of all charges in the first trial, then they should not be indicted for most of the same charges again.

To prove their point, the attorneys began reading the charges in the first indictment and comparing them to the charges in the second indictment. After three days, the trial judge called a halt to the proceedings. Then, in an announcement that surprised even the defense attorneys, he acquitted all the defendants on the second indictment and ordered that they be freed.

Winnie sat in the courtroom so stunned that at first she could not move. In fact, once she did move, she automatically turned in the direction of the courtroom guards, to be taken back to her cell. After sixteen months she was free, but after sixteen months in solitary confinement in Pretoria Central Prison she did not even know what that meant.

Her lawyer escorted her out of the courtroom. Winnie took hesitating steps. Outside, she felt blinded by the sunlight. The cheers of the crowd—relatives and friends and supporters of the accused—seemed deafening. She could not think. She had no plans. But she did know that she must get word to Nelson and her daughters. She had to let them know what had happened.

Winnie later said of her experience in prison, "No human being can go on taking those humiliations without reaction." Some people react to such an experience by turning off all conscious feeling—they never again laugh or cry. They go through the motions of living, but they cease to live. Some of Winnie's supporters worried that this is what would happen to her. But Winnie overcame the humiliations of her prison experience. She would never forget them, but she would not let them make her withdraw from living. After a couple of days rest in her own home, in her own bed, eating her own food, she was ready to live again.

She was also ready to take advantage of the fact that the government had not yet imposed new banning orders on her. During the two weeks or so that it took the government to get around to issuing new orders, she applied for permission to visit Nelson on Robben Island, and she visited her father in the Transkei.

The meeting with her father was very important to her. She had not seen him in many years, and their last communications had been angry ones. Her father was then seventy-seven years old and a member of the cabinet formed for the independent "homeland" of the Transkei, but he no longer believed in the idea of homelands. In fact, he told her that she had been right all along. There was unemployment and overcrowding, and neither industries nor housing to help with these problems. And that didn't even take into account the thousands of blacks from urban areas that the white government was "relocating" to the homelands like the Transkei. Winnie's father had come to understand that "independence" meant nothing without jobs and food and proper housing and medical facilities. The government was using the homelands as dumping grounds for all the blacks it did not want in the white areas.

Winnie felt bad for her father, but she also felt pleased to hear from him that she had been right. She held on to his words, for she'd had so little contact with her family, and so little confirmation that the path she had chosen in life had been the right one.

She desperately needed to be with Nelson, but the government turned down her application to visit him at Robben Island. Many religious and sympathetic political leaders protested to the government about this, and Winnie's second application to visit Nelson was granted.

She traveled to Robben Island for the first time in more than two years. She stepped off the ferry and was escorted into the visitors' building. She watched as her husband was brought to the other side of the glass wall. She wanted so much to run to him and hold him, to have him take her into his arms. But this was not allowed. They spoke through microphones and glass. She told him how sorry she was about Thembi's death. He told her how sorry he was about her long months in prison. He asked about the children, and she told him. All the while, prison guards stood by, listening to their every word, and in the background Winnie could hear the whirr of a tape recorder. Thirty minutes later, their time was up. They looked at each other with longing and painful acceptance of their situation. Winnie felt worse than before she had come. Not long after she returned to her home in Soweto she had a heart attack.

She was only thirty-four years old, but she had been through more ordeals than most people go through in their lifetimes.

·11·

Banished
to Brandfort

*E*ven *before she visited Nelson, Winnie had been served*
with new banning orders from the government. These orders were to be in effect for five years. Among other
things, they provided for her to be under house arrest
every night and during weekends; they also forbade her to
have any visitors.

The security police followed these orders to the letter.
Late in 1970, just weeks after her release from prison, she
was arrested when five relatives visited her, including a
nine-month-old baby and a toddler. The security police
said she had violated her bans against having visitors.
Found guilty in court, she was sentenced to six months'
imprisonment. The sentence was suspended for three years,
and later, after her attorneys appealed, it was set aside.

In 1971, she was arrested for having communication
with a banned person in her house when police raided the
house and found Peter Magubane, the photographer who
was an old friend of the family and the children's god-
father. In court again, Winnie was sentenced to twelve

months' imprisonment, suspended for three years. Again, the conviction and sentence were set aside on appeal.

Winnie's children were with her at the court when sentence was pronounced. Young Zindzi did not understand about the three-year suspension. All she heard was the sentence of twelve months in prison. She burst into tears. Winnie turned on her. "You will never cry in front of a white policeman again!" she told her daughter furiously. Zindzi was only eleven at the time, but her mother knew that she was not too young to put up barriers between her feelings and the outside world. Zindzi never forgot that outburst, and never again let her white enemies know that they had hurt her.

Winnie was constantly harassed, subject to searches at all hours of the night or day, watched all the time by faceless men in unmarked cars that cruised up and down the street or parked across the street at night. Friends brought her a watchdog, and the security police arrested her for allowing them to visit with a dog. Another friend, who also tried to bring her a dog, was arrested for doing so. Not long afterward, the dog was mysteriously killed with poisoned meat.

Since dogs had not worked out very well, friends hired a watchman to guard Winnie's house when she was away from it. But the watchman could do nothing when men flashing security-police badges came around. Winnie returned home to find that all the clothing she had washed and hung out on the clothesline to dry had been slashed with knives.

Another time, a bomb exploded next to the house. And yet another time, burglars sawed through the iron bars on one of her windows, but she could not get the police to make a serious investigation.

Fortunately for Zeni and Zindzi, they were not present when most of these incidents occurred. But they spent enough school holidays with their mother, and witnessed enough such "incidents" to understand that their mother, and they, were being hounded by the security police. In 1972, when she was twelve, Zindzi decided that the only way to protect her mother was to appeal to the international community. She sat down and wrote a letter to the United Nations, pleading for help.

Officials of the United Nations probably get a lot of letters from children asking for help for one reason or another. It is doubtful that the UN people act on most of them. But the Secretary General of the United Nations recognized Zindzi's last name, and in response both he and the International Red Cross asked the South African government to do whatever was possible to assure the safety of Winnie Mandela.

When she learned about it all, Winnie was saddened that Zindzi had felt so powerless and frustrated that she had turned to the UN for help. But at the same time she was grateful to Zindzi for trying and hopeful that perhaps the security police would back off. Unfortunately, the appeals from the international community only served to strengthen the determination of the authorities not to bow to international opinion. Not long afterward, Winnie was arrested for having lunch with her children in the presence of a banned person (Peter Magubane again). She was sentenced to twelve months' imprisonment, suspended for three years.

Winnie tried hard not to spend all her time worrying about the security police. There was no question of her holding a job now, and she had to rely on friends and supporters for money for food and rent. She was watched so closely that she could not engage in any meaningful political activity. At times, she felt that there was nothing left for her to do *but* worry about the police. From time to time, a relative would send her a young niece or nephew or cousin to take care of, and to keep her company—children under ten were supposed to be exempt from the banning orders about visitors. But though Winnie enjoyed taking care of these children, she also worried that they might be caught up in the terrible police attacks that seemed to be a constant part of her life.

In an odd way, everyday human problems were a relief for her to deal with. In 1973 she received word that her father was dying. She applied for and received permission to visit him in the Transkei. She took Zeni and Zindzi with her. Columbus Madikezela insisted on getting dressed up in his best suit, and on standing to receive them, and Winnie loved him for being formal to the end. She understood that he wanted to be remembered as a tall, proud man, and she kissed him for the first time in her life. She had had her differences with him, but she had never lost her love, or her respect, for the man who had taught her so much. She hoped that her children understood, too, that an African man could be a proud man, in or out of prison and in spite of the fact that his ideas might not be the same as theirs.

Not long after her father's death, Winnie's appeal of conviction on her arrest for having lunch with her children in the presence of Peter Magubane came up for judgment. The original sentence of twelve months' imprisonment was reduced to six months. But she had to serve that six months.

Winnie had expected to have to serve at least some time in prison, and she had made arrangements for Zeni and Zindzi, who were home from school on holiday, to be looked after by an elder of her family who lived nearby. It was hard for her to leave the girls, for she saw so little of them as it was, since they were away at school in Swaziland most of the time. She wondered if the State authorities had deliberately chosen school holiday time to sentence her to prison.

She spent the first month at the Johannesburg Fort, where Nelson had been held while awaiting the start of the Treason Trial in 1962. Then, without explanation and in the middle of the night, she was transferred to Kroonstad Prison and placed in a special section with two other women political prisoners. She later described her five months in this prison as a "liberating experience."

The conditions in which she lived were exceptionally good compared to her earlier prison stay. Her daughters were allowed to visit her on Sundays during school vacations. She was provided with clean blankets and prison uniforms, and the food was edible. Each woman had a tiny cell, but they shared a bathroom and a small exercise yard surrounded by high walls. The other women, Dorothy Nyembe and Amina Desai, were as dedicated to the liberation struggle as she was and had endured many hardships, as she had. Dorothy Nyembe was serving fifteen years for harboring guerrilla fighters, and Winnie marveled at her lack of bitterness. Amina Desai was serving a short sentence, and she and Winnie became especially close. From both women, Winnie drew strength and a determination to continue in the struggle.

When her prison sentence was over, Winnie returned home and soon afterward got her first well-paying job since she had been forced to leave the Child Welfare Society. Her employers at the firm Frank and Hirsch refused to be intimidated by the security police, and after a few weeks' time Winnie began to feel that she would be able to stay at the job. She was relieved to be able to pay her own expenses instead of having to rely on friends and benefactors.

In this same year, 1976, Winnie was able to take both Zeni and Zindzi to see their father, for both were over the age of sixteen. Under the law, children between the ages of two and sixteen could not visit prisoners. Zindzi recalled that first visit: "I was a bit apprehensive, I thought . . . this is meant to be my father. What am I going to say? Will he be proud of me? Have I lived up to his standards? But he is such a warm person, and he is so tactful. He said: 'Oh, darling, I can see you now as a kid at home on my lap'—and I immediately forgot the surroundings and we started dreaming and dreaming and then I felt so free; and he has this terrific sense of humour, so it went on so well."

Winnie was nearly as nervous as her daughters. She hoped she had raised the girls in a way that would make the father they had hardly seen proud of them.

In October, six months after her release from prison, Winnie's third banning order expired. She fully expected a new one to be imposed, and was astonished when she was told she was no longer a banned person. For the first time in thirteen years she was actually free to meet with as many people as she wanted, to travel about, to stay out after dark, even to address meetings. But she was not over-grateful to the authorities. As she said at the time, "I am not free. There is no such thing as freedom for me and my people yet. If anything my banning has made me more determined than ever to see change."

She made the most of whatever freedom she had. Forbidden for so long to speak in public, she found it hard to do so at first, but she deliberately sought out opportunities to speak before groups in order to overcome her fear. She traveled to Durban for a reception attended by all races of people who were against apartheid. But she gave most of her public speeches in Soweto, her home township, where unrest was growing, particularly among the young.

The most obvious reason for this unrest was a new government order that students in black secondary schools be taught some subjects in Afrikaans rather than in English. The students already realized that the quality of their education was poor and that they were being deliberately undereducated so as to be unqualified for anything but menial work. They believed that the new regulation would limit their opportunities even more. Also, Afrikaans was the language of their oppressors, and they resented being taught in that language.

At first there were scattered protests. But as the months passed, the students seemed to become more organized. They began staying away from school in large numbers. Their parents were shocked and upset. Most of the parents had little education themselves, and they could not understand why their children would want to throw away the chance at some education, at least. A number of parents sought Winnie's advice, and she called on the authorities to revoke the regulation that was causing so much unrest. Otherwise, she warned, there would be trouble. But the authorities paid her no attention.

In May, Winnie helped to launch the Soweto Parents Association. She and the others who formed the group hoped that the organization might have some influence with the authorities as well as with the students. But already the situation was out of hand. Just a week later, security police went to Naledi High School in Soweto to arrest a student leader. The furious students beat up the two policemen and set fire to their car. The incident was kept quiet by the authorities, who were probably embarrassed about it.

The students now felt a new sense of power. Secretly, they made plans for a huge protest on June 16. Thousands of students wearing their school uniforms would march separately from their schools to a rallying place in Orlando West. They would carry signs and banners reading "Away with Afrikaans" and "We are not Boers." They would sing freedom songs. Winnie and other parents knew that the plans were being made, but the student leaders assured them that the march would be a peaceful one.

On the day of the protest, the police attacked the children as soon as they left their schools. First they ordered them to stop. Then they set dogs on them. And finally they fired upon them. As word of the police action against the children spread through Johannesburg, hundreds of black parents left their jobs and rushed home. Winnie was in her office at Frank and Hirsch when she received a frantic telephone call from a Soweto mother. She ran to her car and raced back to Orlando West.

As she drove through the township, she saw police everywhere, and thousands of determined children. They were carrying trash-can lids to protect themselves from the bullets. But by this time the children were not just defending themselves. The police brutality had unleashed such rage among the students that they had turned into a rampaging mob, stoning cars, smashing windows, setting houses on fire. No one who got in their way was spared, black or white, old or young.

The unrest went on for weeks. During this time fifty government buildings were destroyed. Nearly seventy beer halls and bottle stores were burned to the ground, for the children hated the beer halls for taking their fathers' money. The security police had hoped that the parents would turn on the children because of their violence, but the police violence that had led to the riots had placed the parents solidly on the side of the students.

Winnie, through the Soweto Parents Association, did as much as she could, arranging funerals for the young victims, raising money to pay for coffins, hiding children on the run. When it was all over, at least 600 students, and perhaps more than 1,000, were killed, some of them younger than twelve. Another 4,000 were wounded and several thousand more disappeared, some to safety across the border, others into police detention.

During the weeks of unrest, the violence spread outside Soweto, to nearby Alexandra Township and elsewhere. Winnie urged the formation of a national Black Parents Association to take the lead in fighting for rights instead of letting their children do it. Speaking at a meeting of the Soweto Parents Association, she said, "Not one of the big cities in which we are living today was built without our labor, no railway line without our hands. The country is what it is because of us but now we are driven out of the cities. We carry passes . . . because we cannot marry, rent houses, register births or take a job without passes. Blacks belong to South Africa and it is our right to seek jobs anywhere, but we cannot do so without permits. Our children are now fighting for us while we do nothing."

The authorities accused Winnie of being responsible for the student rioting. "How I wish I did have such powers," she later said. She knew that she was inviting arrest by speaking out, and on August 12 she and other executives of the Soweto Parents Association were arrested under the Internal Security Act. Zeni and Zindzi arrived home for a school holiday to find that she had been taken away.

Winnie was held in solitary confinement for five months in Johannesburg Fort. She was released in January 1977, without ever having been formally charged. Her banning order was renewed for five years.

Fortunately, her job at Frank and Hirsch had been kept open for her. She was able to work there during the day. At night, forbidden to leave her home between 6 P.M. and 6 A.M., she took correspondence courses. By this time her elder daughter, Zeni, had graduated from boarding school. She was soon to marry a Swaziland prince. So it was Zindzi alone who was home on a school holiday and with her mother on May 15, 1977, when the security police banged at the front door, shouting "Open up!" and shone flashlights in the windows. And it was Zindzi who was left alone as her mother was taken away yet again.

While her mother was kept in a cell at Protea Police Station, Zindzi watched horrified as police returned to the Orlando West house, barged in, and began removing all the furniture and clothing and books from the house. Having emptied the house of its contents, they turned to

Zindzi and told her she had a choice: stay in the empty house until she returned to school or accompany her mother to Brandfort. Zindzi didn't even know where Brandfort was, but she knew she wanted to be with her mother.

Meanwhile, Winnie was also asking, "Where is Brandfort?" She had just been served with an order of banishment. She was to be taken to a small village in the Orange Free State, and there she was to live until she was allowed to return home.

Usually when a person was banished, it was to his or her home village. But Brandfort was a world away from Pondoland. The people there didn't even speak Xhosa, and this was exactly what the authorities wanted. They wanted Winnie so far away that she could not influence events in Soweto; and they wanted her in a place so remote and foreign that she also could not influence the people there.

Soon Winnie and her daughter were on their way to Brandfort. The trip took hours, and the farther away from Johannesburg they went the more barren and drab the landscape became. Brandfort was at the end of nowhere, a tiny town divided into a white enclave and a black township that had no name, but that its inhabitants called Phatakele (Handle With Care). The black section was strewn with garbage. There was no plumbing. Water came from a communal tap. The tiny house that was to be her home had no electricity, running water, or sewage system. There was a small outhouse in back. The floors were dirt; there were no shelves for her books. The one door was so narrow that almost none of her furniture would fit through it. Eventually the moving men gave up and took Winnie's furniture to be stored at the police station. Her refrigerator was also plugged in there.

The authorities had told her that she would receive 100 rand a month, from which the rent for the house would be deducted. Winnie had told them to keep their money. She didn't know where she was going to get money, but she did not want it from the government. She was surprised and grateful when her employers at Frank and Hirsch not only sent her her salary for the month of May but continued to send her 250 rand a month for a year. With this money she was able to buy narrow furniture that would fit through her door and other necessities.

Friends sent her money and food. Some of them made the long journey to Brandfort to visit her. She was so grateful to them, but when they left she could barely keep up her spirits.

Winnie had never felt so alone. Her neighbors avoided her. Later she found out that a week before her arrival the local Bantu Authority had told the people that a dangerous woman was coming and that they should have nothing to do with her. Even those who seemed willing to talk with her could not, for they spoke Sotho and Tswana and she spoke Xhosa and English. Winnie realized that the first thing she had to do was to learn their languages.

She did learn their languages, and once she had she began to work to make their lives better. More than ever before, she now called upon her training in social work to help her. She wrote to a friend, "In my childhood in the Transkei I lived among poverty; in my social work in Johannesburg I saw even worse poverty, but never in my life had I imagined conditions as grim as those in this Brandfort ghetto."

There was rampant malnutrition. Women and children scavenged for food scraps in the garbage. Mothers could not afford milk and fed their children a paste of flour and water. Not a week passed without the funeral of a baby. Some of the women had jobs working as domestics in white homes, but they were paid so poorly that they were little better off than those who were unemployed. They brought their midday meal of porridge and oil home at night, so their families might have something to eat.

If children did not starve to death, they often died of simple injuries that went untreated. Winnie made her first real contact with her neighbors when she treated a child who had cut her foot on a broken bottle. After that, she began to talk to the women about hygiene and nutrition.

She herself refused to give in to the squalor around her. She was constantly in trouble for going to the communal water tap after 6 P.M., when she was supposed to be inside her house. Each time she was arrested for this violation, she complained that she was being denied the basic human necessity to wash. So often was she arrested over this that she didn't even keep track of the number of arrests. Meanwhile the authorities were frustrated at her continued resistance. They also noticed that every time she went to the communal water tap at night, many of her neighbors decided to go and get some water as well. They worried that the tap was becoming a place for her to congregate with her neighbors. Finally they decided that the only thing to do was to connect the water source to a tap outside her kitchen. Winnie was delighted to have forced them to provide her, the "dangerous woman," with a luxury that her obedient neighbors did not enjoy. Naturally she offered the use of her tap to all her neighbors.

In time she gained the trust of many of them. She helped them plant small gardens. She even set up a medical clinic. By her example she also taught them, who had never made any demands, to begin to demand things like decent wages and living conditions. And she shocked everyone in the area by refusing to use the special entrance to the police station reserved for nonwhites.

In the course of her stay at Brandfort, Winnie also made friends with a white Afrikaner woman. Adele de Waal was the wife of Brandfort's only attorney, Piet de Waal. Not long after her arrival in Brandfort, Winnie realized that she would need an attorney to represent her against the constant harassment by the authorities. The only attorney available was Piet de Waal. The de Waals had never before dealt with a black except as a servant, but Winnie won them over. Soon Piet de Waal was representing her, and his wife was bringing her food and books and allowing her to use their bathroom for bathing. The de Waals lost friends because of their relationship with Winnie, but they regarded her friendship as far more valuable than that of the friends they lost.

During Winnie's first year at Brandfort, she received word that Zeni would marry Prince Thumbumuzi Dhlamini of Swaziland. Winnie applied for permission to go to Swaziland for the wedding, but her application was denied. Eventually, the Prince's father, King Sobhuza, approached the South African government with a request that the mother of the bride be allowed to attend the wedding. The government granted the King's request.

Meanwhile, the Prime Minister of the Transkei had also asked the South African government to allow Winnie to visit the Transkei in order to attend to family business connected with the wedding. This request, too, was granted by the South African government. The previous year, the Transkei had been granted "independence" as a separate Bantu homeland, and the South African government had little choice but to honor the request of an official of an independent state. The Prime Minister of the Transkei just happened to be Kaiser Matanzima, who had wooed and failed to win Winnie many years earlier.

So Winnie got to go to the Transkei and visit her relatives, and to Swaziland to see her elder daughter married. While as a woman she had no say in the negotiations or preparations surrounding the wedding, she put that resentment aside. She was glad to be out of Brandfort. And she was pleased that she had been able to raise her elder daughter and see her married. But she wished so much that Nelson could have been part of it all.

She also wished that her husband could share in the growth and maturity of their younger daughter, Zindzi. Zindzi had been too young to know her father before he was imprisoned, but she was turning out to be very much like him. She had begun writing poetry at Waterford School, and many of her poems were against the apartheid system in South Africa. In 1978 a collection of her poems was published, with photographs by Peter Magubane, the old friend of the family. Zindzi dedicated the book to her parents, and the first poem in the book was about her father. The book was awarded a prize in the Janusz Korczak Literary Competition, which was established to honor books about children that were examples of selflessness and human dignity. The South African government denied Zindzi a passport, and so she could not go to New York to accept the award. Peter Magubane accepted it on her behalf.

·12·

Changes Coming

*W*innie returned to Brandfort from Swaziland all too soon. Her brief time of freedom had been like a tonic for her, but going back to the drabness and loneliness of Brandfort was made all the more difficult as a result. She refused to become depressed, however, and determined to make a contribution to her people by helping her neighbors in Brandfort.

Her own garden and the lawn she had planted at the front of her home were an inspiration to the others. Half the children in the neighborhood installed themselves on her green grass, and after a while others planted grass in their yards. More and more people came to her for treatment of minor illnesses. Quite a few of them, especially the old, suffered from malnutrition more than anything else, and Winnie decided to open a soup kitchen. When friends wrote to ask what they could send her, she said packets of dried soup. Black Sash, an organization of white women dedicated to the overthrow of apartheid, sent her huge sacks of soup powder.

One day, while shopping in Brandfort, she saw poor black people buying bread by the slice because they could not afford to buy half a loaf. This gave her the idea to teach the women how to bake bread. They learned, and even opened their own bakery to serve the neighborhood. It was a great success.

Then she started a sewing group. She was not able to demonstrate sewing techniques to a group of people, because that would have violated her banning order. So she sat at the back of the Methodist church hall, where the group met, and instructed the women one by one. Now, when people wrote or visited and wanted to know how they could help, she told them she needed fabric and sewing equipment. With donations, she managed to get six sewing machines and a big bolt of cloth. The women used the cloth to make school uniforms for their children.

Winnie Mandela was a one-woman social service center! She took in orphans and delinquents. She treated the sick. She wrote letters to various government agencies on behalf of people who could not read or write. She ran the soup kitchen, the sewing classes, taught nutrition and hygiene. All the while, she studied for an advanced degree in social science from the University of South Africa. Unfortunately, she could not complete the course. To earn the degree she had to do fieldwork, and her banning orders prohibited her from traveling away from Brandfort to do it. She felt that Brandfort was an ideal place to do fieldwork, but officials of the university did not agree. Knowing that it was useless to try to get them to change their minds, Winnie switched to courses in politics and communications. But she could not understand how they could possibly deny that the black township in Brandfort was a place of incredibly primitive conditions.

In spite of the help she received from all over the world, Winnie Mandela herself lived in primitive conditions. She had obtained a refrigerator in her home, powered by paraffin. Thanks to the German ambassador to South Africa, she even had a television, which ran on a huge battery. She loved having neighbors in to watch it, though she had to stay in another room while they did, so as not to violate her banning orders about meeting with groups. She had adequate food, though she was likely to share it with her neighbors and go without herself. And she knew all about hygiene. Still, there was only so much she could do under the conditions in which she was forced to live.

In 1982 she injured her leg, and her own home remedies were not enough. She realized that it was not getting better, but she did not want to go to the white doctors in town. In October, her attorney, Piet de Waal, visited her with some papers he wanted her to sign. He found her feverish and obviously very ill. He sent for a white doctor from Brandfort, who gave her emergency treatment, but the doctor said she should go to a hospital. He believed that her problem had been brought on by the conditions in which she had to live and that she could not be cured if she remained in those same conditions.

Winnie refused to go to the white hospital in Bloemfontein, the nearest city. She insisted on being taken to Johannesburg. Both the doctor and her attorney tried to persuade her to go to Bloemfontein, but Winnie said she would rather die than do that. De Waal contacted the authorities, and they gave in to Winnie's demands. They were afraid that if Winnie did die, they would be blamed for refusing her proper treatment. Winnie was taken to Johannesburg.

Flown to Rosebank Clinic, a private hospital that did not need special permission to admit nonwhites, she was operated on for an infected leg. She then spent seven weeks in the hospital recuperating. After that, though she was still too weak to be returned to Brandfort, the authorities insisted on it.

Her Johannesburg attorney drove her to the airport, only to find that all the seats on the plane to Bloemfontein had been booked. Not knowing what else to do, he turned the car around and drove Winnie to her old home in Orlando West. The authorities warned that if she stayed there she would be violating her banning orders, but they did not remove her. Winnie recuperated in her own home.

Hundreds of Sowetans visited her there, one by one so she would not be accused of meeting groups. They strode right past the security police, who watched the house day and night and who made it their business to take down the names of all who came there. Winnie was astonished by the boldness of the people. She had been away for more than five years, and in that time a great change in attitude had come over Sowetans. They were no longer afraid of the police. Winnie had tried to keep up with political events, but even she was amazed at the new attitude.

The changes had started in 1980. In that year, after a long civil war, Rhodesia's white minority government gave in to the cry for independence by its majority black population. Under British supervision, the first nationwide, free elections were held, pitting leaders of various black factions against one another for control of a new government. South

Africa supported the candidacy of Bishop Abel Muzorewa, and spent a great deal of money on his behalf. But when the votes were counted, the leader of one of the rebel guerrilla groups, Robert Mugabe, had won. Rhodesia became Zimbabwe, an independent black state, and South Africa and Namibia became the last countries on the continent dominated by white minority governments.

Blacks in South Africa were renewed in their hope that the white government there could be toppled, too. And it was not just blacks who felt this way. After decades of quiet, the Cape Coloureds began to rise up in protest. Their students boycotted classes against the Bantu Education laws. In Johannesburg, blacks employed in major industries also went out on strike.

The police, as usual, cracked down hard on the protesters, and there were thousands of arrests and detentions. But in the face of such police brutality, the leaders of black labor unions called for strikes and shut down the mines. This really frightened the authorities, for the mines, with their gold and diamonds and precious minerals, were the lifeblood of the country.

Prime Minister P. W. Botha, who had succeeded B. J. Vorster in 1978, was an Afrikaner who was firmly committed to "separate development" (shipping blacks off to homelands), but as the 1980s dawned he did begin to feel that he was going to have to make some concessions to the restive nonwhites in the country, not to mention the liberal whites who believed that some of the apartheid laws must be repealed.

He urged modest reforms. In 1982, white South Africans voted in a new constitution that created separate chambers of Parliament for Indians and Coloureds. It also created a new, top government position of Executive President with wide powers. Botha then abolished the position of Prime Minister and named himself Executive President.

Elections were held for the new nonwhite chambers of Parliament. But neither Indians nor Coloureds participated in large numbers. They called them a farce, and with good reason—for these chambers of Parliament were not equal in power to the White chamber. Only 20 percent of registered Indian voters and 30 percent of registered Coloured voters even bothered to vote. There was no special chamber for blacks. Winnie called this attempt at political "reform" without including blacks "the best recipe for the worst violence, the worst possible confrontation between blacks and whites."

Under Botha, some of what are called "petty apartheid" laws were revoked. For example, most theaters and restaurants in the major cities were desegregated, as was the Main Public Library in Johannesburg. There were a few "international" hotels in these cities that were integrated. Most of the coaches on South African trains were integrated in 1985, although a few coaches remained for Whites Only.

But these were surface changes that had little effect on the lives of most blacks, who could not afford theater tickets or international hotel rates, and whose limited education kept them from using the public library. Meanwhile, the process of forcibly removing whole townships full of people to the homelands, and bulldozing the townships to rubble, continued. And the laws designed to keep blacks in the townships were made more strict. In 1982, the amount of time a black resident of a homeland could spend in an urban township was reduced from seventy-two hours to seventeen. The punishment for employing an illegal black worker was made even stiffer.

Blacks understood that life was not being made easier for them at all, but harder. The government had no intention of allowing them to be equal citizens of South Africa, and its stubborn plans to make the majority of them live in so-called independent homelands that were incapable of being economically self-supportive infuriated them. They stepped up their protests.

In the course of these protests, the name Nelson Mandela was often heard. The protesters carried placards with his picture on them; his words were frequently quoted. As long as he had been imprisoned, he had never been forgotten by his people. He was their hero, more than Oliver Tambo, leader of the ANC in exile, more than any other leader who had come along since. The black people firmly believed that eventually he would lead them to a new South Africa, in which power was shared among the races. Not just in South Africa, but around the world, there was an active Free Mandela campaign.

Meanwhile, the object of all this respect and devotion seemed to live on the determination to do just what his supporters hoped. People who visited him marveled at how physically and psychologically powerful he was, despite his long years in prison. In his early sixties now, he was strong and fit, and his mind was sharp. He had not let the authorities wear him down with their petty harassments. In fact, he had spent his time worrying not about himself, but about others.

As Winnie had done in Brandfort, Nelson had reached out to his fellow prisoners on Robben Island. Many students arrested in connection with the Soweto uprising had been sent there. Nelson had urged them to continue their studies through correspondence courses. He was so determined that they do so that Robben Island became known unofficially as Mandela University. Young men who had left school in the equivalent of the sixth grade had university degrees by the time they were released from Robben Island.

He commanded even the respect of his guards. A friend who visited him at Robben Island later reported that when the guards had objected to his sharing some sandwiches with Mandela, Mandela had said, "I'm not even prepared to debate this issue with you!"

Perhaps this was why the authorities decided to transfer him from Robben Island to Pollsmoor Maximum Security Prison on the mainland, some miles from Cape Town. They did not like the idea that he had become a sort of Grand Old Man of Robben Island. They may have uncovered, or suspected, some sort of plot to free Mandela. Whatever their reasons, Mandela did not like the change.

Instead of having a cell of his own, he shared one with five other prisoners, and they were isolated from the rest of the prisoners. They had only a small, high-walled exercise yard, and Nelson could no longer garden or take long walks as was his custom.

And yet, at Pollsmoor Prison, Nelson Mandela also was allowed more family visits. The reason may have been political. Zeni was, after all, married to a member of the royal family of Swaziland, and the South African authorities wished to accord her diplomatic treatment. Suddenly, Zeni and her husband and new baby were allowed a "contact visit." Zeni recalls, "He had never held a baby for sixteen years. He had seen us but never touched us. I thought he would break down."

On the weekend of May 12-13, 1984, Winnie was finally allowed a contact visit with her husband. She arrived at Pollsmoor with Zeni and Zeni's youngest child, and was asked to go to the office of a Sergeant Gregory. Winnie immediately got worried, fearing that Nelson was ill. But the sergeant told her that from now on she would have "different visits." He wanted to break the news to her gently. What he meant was that after twenty-two years she and her husband would be allowed to touch.

"We kissed Nelson and held him a long time," Winnie later recalled. She did not say much else about how she felt, except that it was not possible to describe. It was easier for her to talk about the feelings of the guard who witnessed the event. "Gregory, his warder, was so moved, he looked the other way. That the system could have been so cruel as to deny us that right for the last twenty-two years!"

Nelson was now allowed thirty visits from family per year. Winnie and her daughters used them all.

By this time, both Zeni and Zindzi were in their middle twenties, and each in her own way had taken up her parents' struggle. Zeni, who was free to travel wherever she wanted, often accepted international awards on behalf of her father and mother and used these occasions to speak out against the brutal oppression of blacks in South Africa. Zindzi was deeply involved in the struggle against apartheid in South Africa. In 1980, on the twentieth anniversary of the Sharpeville massacre, in which police firing into a crowd of demonstrators had killed sixty-nine and wounded 180 blacks, she spoke to a large gathering of white students at the University of Witwatersrand, saying,

"I have not joined you as a daughter calling for the release of her father. I have joined as part of my generation who have never known a normal life."

By early 1985, it was clear that the South African government of President P. W. Botha wanted to make some sort of major concession to the country's blacks, or at least to the growing number of people and governments in the world that urged him to do something. A group called the International League of Human Rights called for Mandela's release. Other human rights organizations called for an end to apartheid. Eight years earlier, in 1977, a black minister in the United States, the Reverend Leon Sullivan, had come up with a list of principles that he wanted American companies doing business in South Africa to follow. These Sullivan Principles included giving native black South Africans jobs in management wherever possible and making efforts not to further the cause of apartheid. Many big companies had signed these principles.

On U. S. college campuses there were demonstrations against apartheid and against companies that did business in South Africa. Many universities and municipalities sold their stock in these companies. In the U.S. Congress there was talk of imposing economic sanctions on South Africa—laws prohibiting U.S. companies from investing or doing business there, laws preventing U.S. airlines from flying to South Africa and South African airlines from landing in the U.S. Other countries imposed sanctions or talked about doing so.

Botha faced serious economic problems if he did not do something, and it seemed to him that releasing Nelson Mandela might take some of the pressure off his country and his government. On January 31 Botha announced that his government would consider releasing Mandela on the condition that he give a commitment that he would not "make himself guilty of planning, instigating or committing acts of violence for the furtherance of political objectives." The other men convicted in the Rivonia Trial received the same offer.

On February 10, 1985, Nelson and Winnie's daughter, Zindzi, read her father's reply to a huge crowd assembled at Soweto's Jubulani Stadium. It read in part:

"Let [Botha] renounce violence. Let him say that he will dismantle apartheid. Let him unban the people's organization, the African National Congress. Let him free all who have been imprisoned, banished or exiled for their opposition to apartheid. Let him guarantee free political activity so that the people may decide who will govern them. . . .

"I am not less life-loving than you are. But I cannot sell my birthright, nor am I prepared to sell the birthright of the people to be free. I am in prison as the representative of the people and of your organization, the African National Congress, which was banned. What freedom am I being offered while the organization of the people remains banned? What freedom am I being offered when I may be arrested on a pass offense? What freedom am I being offered to live my life as a family with my dear wife, who remains in banishment in Brandfort? . . .

"I cannot and will not give any undertaking at a time when I and you the people are not free. Your freedom and mine cannot be separated. I will return."

It took every ounce of courage that Nelson Mandela possessed to renounce the chance for freedom. And it took every ounce of courage that Winnie Mandela possessed to support him. Neither of them wanted to remain apart, and neither of them wanted him to stay in prison after so many years. But both refused to be used by the white South African government, and that is what the government was offering. The government hoped that Nelson would renounce violence and stop being such a potent symbol of freedom to his people. If he renounced violence and left prison, he would be just a man again, or so the government hoped. Nelson Mandela refused to be used. And so did his wife.

Winnie was approached by government representatives who suggested that if she cooperated with them, she might help her husband's cause. But she would not cooperate with them. "Nelson's release, on its own, is not the issue," she declared. "We are struggling for the freedom of our people."

After so many years of hardship, Winnie Mandela was not about to accept crumbs from the table of the white rulers when she firmly believed that her people were entitled to the whole loaf of bread, as well as the table.

Black unrest continued, and grew. Now, young blacks in the urban townships would answer to no one. They had developed their own organizations and their own ways of fighting back, and they did not care to listen to their parents or to leaders of the older organizations. They called each other "comrade" and followed their ideas of what Communism was all about. They hated blacks who cooperated with the white authorities as much as they hated the white authorities themselves, and because they could reach the black cooperators more easily than the whites, they took out their fury on them. Throughout the spring of 1985 there were riots in the townships, and many suspected black collaborators were killed by the horrifying "necklace." This was a tire filled with gasoline, placed around the neck of the victim, and ignited. Hundreds of black township officials were killed in this way. In the middle of June the government actually promised to stop the forcible removal of blacks from townships to the homelands, but the removals continued. So did the riots. ANC pamphlets became more demanding and confident in their tone.

In July 1985, the government declared a state of emergency in some forty black districts. Among other things, it gave the security police even greater authority to detain and hold without formal charges anyone regarded as suspicious and imposed stricter curfews. But this did little to stop the violence in the black townships, and once again the government approached Nelson Mandela with the idea of releasing him if he would renounce violence. Winnie announced her husband's rejection of the offer: "The only thing that is left to be discussed by the people of this country and the ruling Afrikaners is the handing over of power to the majority," she quoted him as saying.

On August 14, 1985, young black demonstrators in Brandfort were set upon by police and sought refuge in Winnie's house. Police used rubber bullets and whips to ferret them out. They also set fire to Winnie's house and clinic. Winnie announced that since her house in Brandfort was no longer fit to live in, she was going to her home in Orlando West. The government reminded her that she would thus be violating her banishment order, but she paid no attention. She went to Soweto.

Winnie believed that the time had come to defy the government. Not only did she go to her home in the township outside Johannesburg, she further defied her banning orders by speaking out in public and attending funerals and demonstrations. The government now threatened to curb her visits to her husband, but Winnie refused to back down. As she had expected, the government did not carry through its threats.

To the rest of the world, Winnie Mandela became a major presence. Her picture was constantly in the newspapers, and so were her antigovernment and antiapartheid statements. The South African government still controlled its country's newspapers and press, however, and forbade them to quote her or show her picture. And thus it was not any public statements by Winnie Mandela that incited Cape Town schoolchildren to battle police in late August.

To the rest of the world, it looked as if P. W. Botha was going to have to make some major concessions to keep his country from exploding. When it was announced that he would make a major policy speech, many hoped that he would at last offer at least limited political participation to blacks. But Botha's speech contained no such concessions. In fact, he announced that the policies of moving most blacks to separate homelands would continue.

Winnie continued to defy her banishment orders and stayed in Orlando West. The U.S. Embassy in South Africa offered her $10,000 for the reconstruction of her home in Brandfort, but she refused the offer, saying that she would accept nothing from a government that "echoes the programs of a racist regime." She also continued to attend public events and to speak out in public. In early December 1985, she attended a mass funeral for victims of police violence; and in the rally afterward outside Pretoria, attended by 2,000, she announced, "The day is not far when we shall lead you to freedom. In the same way as you have had to bury your children today, so shall the blood of these heroes we buried today be avenged."

About two weeks later, the government offered her renewed and relaxed restrictions on her movements. These included allowing her to attend social gatherings, and to leave Brandfort without having to report to police stations wherever she went. She would still be barred from living in Soweto, from attending political meetings, from being quoted, from entering educational institutions, from distributing publications or joining political movements. The documents outlining these new restrictions were delivered to Winnie at her home in Orlando West, but she refused to accept them. The police then asked her to go with them, and she refused to do that as well. Two policemen, each taking an arm, picked her up bodily and dragged her out of the house. Naturally, once this was reported in the international press, the authorities lost all chance of appearing willing to be more lenient with Winnie Mandela.

Once again the government backed down. Winnie was released, and over the next few months she continued to defy her banishment orders. In April 1986, she was quoted for the first time in two South African newspapers. She urged greater black defiance of apartheid laws. In July, her bans were formally lifted, but she had paid no attention to them for months anyway.

During all his long years in prison, Nelson Mandela had managed to keep abreast of the current news, and he must have been exceptionally proud of Winnie. She was speaking out, defying a government whose authority she did not accept. She was risking her own safety, but refusing to be bowed. She had become, in her own right, the Mother of the Black Nation, just as he was the Father.

· 13 ·

Dream of a Nation

By the summer of 1986, worldwide opposition to apartheid was overwhelming. The U.S. Congress voted to cut off investment in South Africa. More and more international companies were pulling out. Black African countries, which had been afraid to cut economic ties with South Africa because their own economies depended heavily on that country, began to find ways around that economic dependence.

Faced with such worldwide opposition, the South African government imposed severe press restrictions. Now the foreign press was effectively barred from reporting on what was going on in South Africa. Many foreign reporters were expelled from the country for defying the new restrictions, and it became difficult for people in the rest of the world to know what was going on. Meanwhile the people of South Africa had long been kept from knowing the real state of affairs because internal press censorship had been going on for years. But world pressure did not stop. More and more sanctions were imposed on South

Africa. And internal pressure did not stop either. Many whites—English and Afrikaners—were convinced that a bloodbath was in store for South Africa. Some left the country, the majority of them reportedly going to Australia. Others began to push for a relaxation of the apartheid laws before it was too late. Still others, mainly Afrikaners, took an even harder line against blacks, recalling the time more than a century ago when the Voortrekkers pulled their wagons in a circle and fought off the Zulu. The extreme press censorship was a kind of wagon-circling tactic.

In the parliamentary elections of May 1987, that circle of wagons was tightened even more. President Botha's National Party was returned to Parliament with a greater majority than it had enjoyed before, and more members of the Conservative Party, which is even less willing to consider rights for blacks, were voted in. The Liberal Party, which is most friendly to black demands for an end to apartheid, lost seats in Parliament.

There had been much black unrest in the weeks leading up to the elections—work stoppages and strikes and protests. Apparently this unrest had only hardened the resolve of many voters. Blacks who had hoped the elections would result in a loss of strength for the Nationalists and Conservatives saw them as a further slap in the face. What Winnie Mandela thought about it all is not publicly known, for the severe press restrictions in South Africa prevented her from being quoted. But anyone who knew what she stood for also knew how she felt.

Still, less than two months after the elections, she could again find some reason to keep her hopes alive. World opinion against South Africa hardened in the face of the stiff resistance of white South Africans who did not want change. The Reverend Leon Sullivan, author of the 1977 Sullivan Principles for American companies doing business in South Africa, announced that he had changed his mind. He no longer believed that apartheid could be brought down by working within the system. American companies in South Africa had hired and promoted black workers and otherwise followed his fair-employment principles, but that had done no good for the mass of black people. Sullivan now called for U.S. companies to leave South Africa.

Shortly afterward two major American companies did so, although both denied that there was any connection with Sullivan's announcement. One was the Ford Motor Company. The other was Citibank, one of the largest banks in the world and the only U.S.-owned bank that was still doing business in South Africa. These moves heartened those who were against apartheid, although they knew that neither the economy nor the government would topple as a result.

Meanwhile, South Africa's blacks continued to dream of a time when they would exercise power equivalent to their numbers. There are some who dream of driving out all the whites. And there are many more who dream of a nation like Zimbabwe, where blacks and whites have managed to live, and govern, together. Nelson and Winnie Mandela are among them. They dream of a nation where people of all colors share power, and respect for one another. In January 1985, Nelson Mandela explained to Samuel Dash, a member of the International League of Human Rights, "Unlike white people anywhere else in Africa, whites in South Africa belong here—this is their home.

We want them to live here with us and share power with us."

Winnie has made fewer remarks like that. She is more militant than her husband. But she has also, in some ways, had a harder time than her husband. At this writing, she is still being awakened in the middle of the night and hauled off for questioning at police stations. She is still experiencing, on a day-to-day basis, the inhuman treatment that blacks receive in South Africa.

While she eventually came to share with her husband the belief that the struggle comes first, she fell in love with a man, not a movement, and she cannot help feeling some bitterness that she has been forcibly separated from him for so many years and that her children grew up never really knowing their father. She has had to endure great hardship and the loss of many loved ones over the years, from her sister Vuyelwa and her mother when she was young to, more recently, her father, her stepson Thembi, her beloved sister Nancy, who died in exile of leukemia in 1980, and in early 1985, her younger sister Nikiwe Xaba, in an accident.

On learning of Nikiwe's death, Nelson wrote to Winnie, "On occasions like this I often wonder just how far more difficult it would have been for me to take the decision to leave you behind if I had been able to see clearly the countless perils and hardships to which you would be exposed in my absence. I sincerely think that my decision would, nonetheless, have been easily the same, but it would certainly have been preceded by far more heart-searching and hesitation than was the case twenty-four years ago. . . . Your love and support . . . the charming children you have given the family, the many friends you

have won, the hope of enjoying that love and warmth
again, is what life and happiness mean to me. . . . Yet
there have been moments when that love and happiness,
that trust and hope, have turned into pure agony, when
conscience and a sense of guilt have ravaged every part of
my being, when I have wondered whether any kind of
commitment can ever be sufficient excuse for abandoning
a young and inexperienced woman in a pitiless desert,
literally throwing her into the hands of highwaymen; a
wonderful woman without her pillar and support in times
of need."

In her reply to that letter, Winnie told her husband that
it had reconstructed her shattered soul. She also told him
how she sometimes dreamed of meeting him on the steps
of Pollsmoor Prison and being told to take him home. At
this writing, that is still a dream, as distant and impossible
as is the dream of nationhood for black South Africans.

World pressure, both moral and economic, against
apartheid continues to increase. Bishop Desmond Tutu,
Anglican Archbishop of Cape Town, a black South African who is committed to nonviolence, was awarded the
Nobel Prize for Peace in 1984. More and more countries
have voted sanctions of some kind against South Africa.
Inside South Africa, the number of liberal whites willing
to speak out against apartheid has grown. In January 1986,
Dr. Frederick van Zyl Slabbert, the leader of the liberal
white opposition to the Botha party in Parliament, re-
signed from the whites-only chamber of Parliament,
charging that parliamentary debate that excluded the
black majority had become "a ritual of irrelevance." He
formed the Institute for Democratic Alternatives for South
Africa, which seeks to create an atmosphere favorable to

negotations between blacks and whites. In 1987 world-famous Afrikaner golfer Gary Player spoke out against apartheid. More and more intellectuals and businessmen have done the same.

But the diehard supporters of apartheid have also become more outspoken. In fact, many of them believe that Botha has been too willing to compromise and hasn't taken a sufficiently hard line. It is these people whom Helen Suzman, a white woman and a member of Parliament from the Progressive Federal Party who has long been an antiapartheid activist, feels most concerned about. She disagrees with some outside observers that economic sanctions against South Africa will bring about a change in attitude among these diehards. Most of them cannot afford to move to Australia. A sizable number of them hold government jobs which they would stand to lose if blacks had an equal share in the government. Most of them regard themselves as strong patriots whose responsibility it is to keep alive the memory of the Voortrekkers. Each time changes seem possible, these stubborn Afrikaners who resist all change dig their heels in deeper, circle their wagons more closely, and refuse to budge.

There may come a time when the fate of South Africa will be decided in a pitched battle between these wagon-circling whites and the necklace-wielding young urban blacks. But it is unlikely that either Nelson or Winnie Mandela will be around to see it happen.

At this writing, Nelson Mandela is nearly seventy years old, Winnie is in her early fifties. They still command the allegiance and respect of the majority of blacks, not to mention Coloureds and some Indians and liberal whites, and this is nothing short of remarkable considering that he has been in prison for a quarter of a century and she has been either banned or banished for nearly that long. They are symbols to their people, and they accept that existence. Both have put aside their own lives and personal dreams in order to work for their people, and having devoted half their lives or more to the struggle, they have no choice but to continue. They know that when they are gone, a younger generation of activists will carry on the struggle. Their younger daughter, Zindzi, will be among them. Zindzi has chosen to study law, as her father did, and to be an outspoken antiapartheid activist like both her parents. Thus, she faces the same kind of police harassment that plagues her mother. In February 1987, she was detained by security police and questioned for several hours after police raided the Mandela home in Soweto and claimed to have found a gun "on top of her cupboard." Nelson and Winnie Mandela must have mixed feelings about Zindzi's activism—proud of her courage and commitment but sad that she faces a life as hard as theirs has been.

Both Nelson and Winnie Mandela are heroes of a kind rarely seen in human history. They are unique also because they are husband and wife. And Winnie Mandela is special because of what she has had to battle and overcome as a woman—not just family and society but the forces of a determined and brutal government—in order to make her own choices and follow her own destiny.

Bibliography

Books

Benson, Mary. *Nelson Mandela: The Man and the Movement* (London and New York: W. W. Norton & Co., 1986).

Finnegan, William. *Crossing the Line: A Year in the Land of Apartheid* (New York: Harper & Row, 1986).

First, Ruth. *Power in Africa* (New York: Pantheon Books, 1970).

Harrison, Nancy. *Winnie Mandela* (New York: George Braziller, Inc., 1986).

Jenkins, Geoffrey, and Eve Palmer. *The Companion Guide to South Africa* (London: William Collins & Co., Inc., 1978).

Lelyveld, Joseph. *Move Your Shadow: South Africa, Black and White* (New York: Times Books, 1985).

Mandela, Winnie. *Part of My Soul Went With Him* (New York: W. W. Norton & Co., Inc., 1985).

Mathabane, Mark. *Kaffir Boy: The True Story of a Black Youth's Coming of Age in South Africa* (New York: Macmillan Publishing Co., 1986).

Meyer, Carolyn. *Voices of South Africa: Growing Up in a Troubled Land* (San Diego: Harcourt Brace Jovanovich, 1986).

Periodicals

African Concord
The Christian Science Monitor
Current Biography, January 1986
The Detroit Free Press
The London Times
Newsweek
The New York Times
Time
The Toronto Star
U.S. News & World Report
The Weekly Mail (Johannesburg)

Index